Ralegh's Country

The South West of England in the Reign of Queen Elizabeth I

by

Joyce Youings

Raleigh

America's Four Hundredth Anniversary Committee
North Carolina Department of Cultural Resources

1986

America's Four Hundredth Anniversary Committee

Lindsay C. Warren, Jr.
Chairman

Marc Basnight
Andy Griffith
John P. Kennedy
Robert V. Owens, Jr.

William S. Powell
L. Richardson Preyer
S. Thomas Rhodes
Harry Schiffman
Mrs. J. Emmett Winslow

David Stick
Mrs. Percy Tillett
Charles B. Wade, Jr.
Charles B. Winberry, Jr.

John D. Neville
Executive Director

Mrs. Marsden B. deRosset, Jr.
Assistant Director

Advisory Committee on Publications

William S. Powell
Chairman

Lindley S. Butler
Jerry C. Cashion
David Stick
Alan D. Watson

ISBN 0-86526-207-1

Copyright 1986
by the
Division of Archives and History
North Carolina Department of Cultural Resources

Contents

Ralegh's Country

The South West of England
in the Reign of Queen Elizabeth I

Maps and Illustrations

Foreword

America's Four Hundredth Anniversary Committee, formed in 1978 under the provisions of an act of the North Carolina General Assembly of 1973, was charged with recommending plans for the observance of the quadricentennial of the first English attempts to explore and settle North America. The committee has proposed to carry out a variety of programs to appeal to a broad range of people. Among these is a publications program that includes a series of booklets dealing with the history of the events and people of the 1580s.

Queen Elizabeth I of England enjoyed a reign that was for the most part peaceful. It was a period of prosperity, which saw the flourishing of a new interest in literature, religion, exploration, and business. English mariners began to venture farther from home, and in time talk began to be heard of hopes to establish naval bases and colonies in America. Men of the County of Devon in the southwest of England, seafarers for generations, played leading roles in this expansion. One of these, Walter Ralegh (as he most often wrote his name), became a favorite of the queen, and on him she bestowed a variety of honors and rewards. It was he to whom she granted a charter in 1584 authorizing the discovery and occupation of lands not already held by "any Christian Prince and . . . people." Ralegh promptly sent a reconnaissance expedition to what is now North Carolina, and this was followed in due time by a colony under the leadership of Ralph Lane. Headquarters were established on Roanoke Island. After remaining for nearly a year and exploring far afield, Lane and his men returned to England in 1586.

In the summer of 1587 Governor John White and a colony of 115 men, women, and children arrived and occupied the houses and the fort left by Lane. The brief annals of this colony are recorded in a journal kept by the governor; they tell of certain problems that arose early—but they also record the birth of the first English child in America. The journal further explains why Governor White consented to return to England for supplies. His departure was the last contact with the settlers who constituted the "Lost Colony," renowned in history, literature, and folklore.

Although a casual acquaintance with the facts of these English efforts might suggest that they were failures, such was far from the case. Ralegh's expenditures of time, effort, and resources (in which he was joined by many others, including Queen Elizabeth herself) had salutary effects for England and certainly for all of present-day America. From Ralegh's initial investment in the reconnaissance voyage, as well as from the colonies, came careful descriptions of the New World and samples of its products. The people of England, indeed of the Western world, learned about North America; because books were published based on what Ralegh's men discovered, they could soon read for themselves of the natives there and the promise of strange and wonderful new resources.

From these voyages and colonizing efforts came the conviction that an English nation could be established in America. In 1606, when another charter was about to be issued for further settlement, King James, who succeeded Queen Elizabeth at her death in 1603, called for advice from some of the men who had been associated with Ralegh. They assured the king that further efforts would surely succeed. With this the Virginia Company was chartered, and it established England's first permanent settlement in America at Jamestown.

Because of Sir Walter Ralegh's vision, England persisted. Because of England's persistence and its refusal to yield to Spain's claims to the region, the United States today enjoys an English heritage. The English common law is the basis of American law; American legislative bodies are modeled on the House of Commons with the rights and freedoms that it developed over a long period of time; America's mother tongue is English, and it is the most commonly spoken language in the world—pilots and navigators on international airlines and the controllers who direct them at airports all over the world use English. Americans also share England's literary tradition: Chaucer, Beowulf, King Arthur, and Shakespeare are America's too, and Americans can enjoy Dickens and Tennyson, as well as Agatha Christie and Dorothy Sayers. America's religious freedom is also in the English tradition, and several of this nation's Protestant denominations trace their earliest history to origins in England: the Episcopal church, certainly, but the Quakers, Baptists, Congregationalists, and Universalists as well.

America's Four Hundredth Anniversary Committee has planned many programs to direct national and even international attention to the significance of events that occurred from bases established by English men, women, and children, but notably Sir Walter Ralegh, in what is now North Carolina during the period 1584-1590. While some of the programs may be regarded as fleeting and soon forgotten, the publications are intended to serve as lasting reminders of America's indebtedness to England. Books, pamphlets, and folders covering a broad range of topics have been prepared by authors on both sides of the Atlantic. These, it is anticipated, will introduce a vast new audience to the facts of America's origins.

Lindsay C. Warren, Jr., *Chairman*
America's Four Hundredth Anniversary Committee

Introduction

At the beginning of May, 1594, a dozen Cornish gentlemen waited upon Sir Walter Ralegh at Sherborne Castle in Dorset. They had joined forces at Exeter for dinner on April 30 and were on their way to London. Only with difficulty did they obtain an audience, being at first received by Ralegh's half brother, Adrian Gilbert, who showed them around the new mansion. They were told that Sir Walter was sick, but they suspected that he was annoyed because one of their party who had preceded them had hinted to Ralegh that they were not expecting much help. Only when they prepared to leave were they admitted to the small chamber where Ralegh lay on a "pallet," or small bed. Their reception was hardly warm, but Sir Walter listened to their story, which concerned certain leases to a stranger of landholdings forming part of the estates of the royal Duchy of Cornwall, in contravention, they claimed, of ancient custom. Ralegh mellowed somewhat, his interest perhaps aroused by the fact that the leases had been made on the authority of the queen's lord treasurer, William Cecil, Lord Burghley. When Ralegh's visitors reminded him that he, as high steward of the duchy, had a duty to act as their friend, Ralegh not only advised them how to proceed at Westminster but also had his secretary pen letters supporting their case. The Cornishmen then proceeded on their journey.

Whether the suit was furthered by Ralegh's support or depended on its own merits or upon the dogged persistence of the Cornishmen, the leases were eventually withdrawn. The whole story was put on record by the leader of the deputation, the well-known Cornish scholar and man of affairs, Richard Carew of Anthony.[1] In dedicating his *Survey of Cornwall* (1602) to Ralegh, Carew paid particular tribute to his patron's constant willingness to further the interests of Cornwall, also mentioning elsewhere in his book the help given by Ralegh, himself no stranger to monopolies, in obtaining the revocation of a royal grant to one Henry Warren to license the salting, drying, and packing of fish throughout Devon and Cornwall.[2] Whether Ralegh was actually in a position to confer this particular benefit may well be doubted, especially as it must have been in 1592 at about the

To the Honourable, Sir Walter
Raleigh *Knight, Lord Warden of the*
Stannaries, Lieutenant Generall of
Cornwall, &c.

His mine ill-husbanded Suruey, long
since begun, a great while discontinu-
ed, lately reuiewed, and now hasti-
ly finished, appealeth to your L.
direction, whether it should passe;
to your correction, if it doe passe; and to your pro·
tection, when it is passed. Neithervnduely: for the
same intreateth of the Prouince, and persons, ouer
whose bodies, and estates, you carrie a large, both
Martiall, and ciuill commaund, by your authoritie,
but in whose hearts, and loues, you possesse a farre
greater interest, by your kindnesse. Your eares, and
mouth, haue euer beene open, to heare, and deliuer
our grieuances, and your feete, and hands, readie to
goe, and worke their redresse, and that, not onely,
alwayes, as a Magistrate, of your selfe, but also verie
often, as a suiter, and solliciter to others, of the high-

¶ 3   est

The Epistle Dedicatorie.

est place. Wherefore, I, as one of the common be-
holden, present this token of my priuate gratitude.
It is dutie, and not presumption, that hath drawne
me to the offering; and it must be fauour, and
not desert, that shall moue your Lordship
to the acceptance: and so I take hum-
ble leaue, resting no lesse willing
to serue you, then
vnder you.

Your Lordships poore kinsman,

Richard Carew of
Antonie.

Shown above is the dedication page of Richard Carew's *Survey of Cornwall* (1602). Carew dedicated the work to Sir Walter Ralegh as a "token of my priuate gratitude." Photograph courtesy University of Exeter.

time that he and his newly wedded wife, Bess Throgmorton, were banished from the court. Indeed, although Carew makes no mention of the fact, Lady Ralegh and baby Damerei must have been somewhere in the house at Sherborne when he and his friends called. The important point is that Ralegh's charisma in the South West was such that the Cornish gentlemen not only sought his help but believed that his support had been crucial.

A study of Ralegh's background and his standing in the region may give insight into the relationship of the people and culture of the Elizabethan South West to the Roanoke voyages of 1584-1587.

I. Ralegh the Devonian

At the time of his marriage, when, unlike most Tudor gentlemen, he was nearly forty years old, Ralegh employed his friend John Hooker of Exeter, an experienced antiquary, to investigate his ancestry. There was no need for fabrication, for Sir Walter possessed what many of his contemporaries would have envied: a genuinely ancient lineage. The parish of Colaton Raleigh, in which his father owned land, had been thus designated for all of 250 years, but this was in east Devon, some ten miles from Exeter and a long way from the hamlet of Raleigh near Barnstaple in north Devon, from which the family had taken its name more than 300 years earlier. The latter had passed by marriage, on the failure, before 1400, of the senior branch of the family, to the Chichesters, ancestors of Sir Francis, the round-the-world yachtsman of the second Elizabethan age. The junior branch, from which Sir Walter was descended, had been seated in the early part of the sixteenth century at Fardell in the parish of Cornwood near Plymouth, which, like most of the family's scattered estates, had been acquired by marriage with an heiress. Some of Sir Walter's direct ancestors had been knights, but for the most part his family had never been more than gentry. The family continued in that condition long after Sir Walter had lived and died, neither his father nor any of his brothers having added permanently to the family's fortunes.

Walter Ralegh senior (1505-1581) had inherited Fardell and the rest of the property while still a minor. His mother had been an Edgcumbe of Cotehele, and an Edgcumbe uncle was one of the trustees of his estate. At about the time of his first marriage in the mid-1520s, to Joan Drake, daughter of John Drake of Axmouth, gentleman, Walter senior had moved to east Devon. He was certainly living in East Budleigh by 1546 and considerably earlier if the bench end in the parish church dated 1537 did once carry the Ralegh arms. His own father had sold Smallridge in Axminster on the Dorset border to John Gilbert of Compton in the parish of Marldon, inland from Torbay, and there was presumably no suitable or vacant residence in Colaton Raleigh or Withycombe Raleigh or the money to build one. Walter and Joan obtained from the Duke family, owners of the manor of

Hayes in the parish of East Budleigh, a lease of the "capital messuage," that is, the barton or principal farm of the manor, including the farmhouse, later called Hayes Barton. The lease of Hayes was certainly before 1551, when it was renewed by Richard Duke to Walter senior and his son, John, for eighty years, terminable with their lives. The rent was £12, plus an additional fifteen pence payable to the lord of Okehampton. The first Ralegh lease may have been acquired from a Henry Kenwood, who in 1527 had obtained from John Duke and his wife, Joan, a lease for sixty years after the death or surrender of a Thomas Isack, who was then in occupation.[3] By 1551 Walter Ralegh senior had lost his first wife, who is commemorated by a stone slab in East Budleigh church; had married and buried a lady from London; and was probably already married to Katherine (née Champernowne), widow of Otho Gilbert of Compton in south Devon, nephew of the purchaser of Smallridge.

Although it is unlikely that all of them lived together at Hayes, the Ralegh family was a large one. By his first wife, Walter had had two sons, George and John, the second of whom married a Fortescue from Filleigh in north Devon. By his second wife he had a daughter, Mary, who married Hugh Snedall, gentleman, of Exeter. Katherine, his third wife, was already the mother of John, Humphrey, and Adrian Gilbert and of a daughter, also Katherine, who may have married Walter's eldest son and heir, George. The third Mistress Ralegh now bore her second husband two more sons—Carew and Walter—the latter almost certainly in 1554, and a daughter, Margaret. To some it may have seemed as if Katherine had disparaged herself by marrying Walter senior, but as a widow she could please herself; and it was almost certainly a real love match, as few Tudor first marriages were. In any case, Walter became a justice of the peace in 1547, an honor very oddly never conferred on Otho Gilbert. But even the Champernownes, as well as the Edgcumbes, the Gilberts, and the Fortescues, although their houses were larger and grander than Hayes, lived in what were only glorified farmhouses, their servants very largely farmhands. The same was true of Stowe, in northeast Cornwall, the house of the Grenvilles. Walter Ralegh senior's brother-in-law, John Drake junior, of Ash in the parish of Musbury, had married Amy Grenville, sister of the Sir Richard with whom young Walter would later be closely associated. John and Amy Drake had a son, Bernard, later knighted, who married Gertrude Fortescue, a sister of the wife of John Ralegh. Another sister married Robert Yeo, esquire, of Heanton Sachville in north Devon, and all of these gentry "cousins" must have been very well known to Walter Ralegh junior during his boyhood.

Hayes was an untypical east Devon farm in that it comprised little or no arable land, but there was meadow and also extensive grazing rights on Woodbury and Lympstone Commons. Indeed, until some time after the birth of his youngest son, Walter Ralegh senior's main occupation was privateering or, if necessary, piracy; and if young Walter ever had the leisure to stare out to sea, it was more likely that he did so from the beach at Exmouth than from Budleigh Salterton. How really profitable the seafaring was is not known. In 1549 Walter senior was accorded the totally unwelcome honor of being included in a list of twenty-six Devon gentlemen thought to enjoy £40 or more in landed income and therefore to be liable to distraint of knighthood, a form of taxation. There is, however, no evidence that he had added at all to his landed property. All the former monastic land in and around East Budleigh was being bought by the Drakes and the Dukes out of small fortunes made in trade and royal service, and indeed by the later 1550s Walter and Katherine were selling parts of their estate, possibly to buy shipping.

In 1555 Walter Ralegh senior became a freeman of Exeter, possibly with a view to securing one of the city's parliamentary seats (he was, in fact, returned for Wareham in Dorset in 1558), and in the mid- or later 1560s he seems to have moved his household into Exeter. In the muster rolls of 1569 his name appears among the city's men of property charged with the provision of armor,[4] and in 1577 he was assessed there for the subsidy, although in 1575 young Walter was enrolled at the Middle Temple as the son of Walter Ralegh "of Budleigh." The old man's funeral was certainly solemnized in the parish church of St. Mary Major in Exeter in 1581. His widow continued to live in their house adjoining Palace Gate in Exeter until her death in 1594. Her will took the form of a letter addressed to her "dear sons," who may or may not have included Walter. They were "earnestly entreated" to "see such debts to be satisfied as shall be demanded after my departure . . . my servants satisfied, and to have their due in such things as I have bestowed upon them to the uttermost farthing, to the end I may end my days towards God with a pure heart and faithful conscience." Katherine Ralegh's debts included the large sum of £8 owed to the butcher and £4 15s owed to her apothecary. To her friend and neighbor, Mistress Katherine Hooker (wife of John's eldest son Richard and daughter of Katherine's stepdaughter Mary, the wife of Hugh Snedall), she left her bed and its furnishing, her saddle and its cloth, a small salt, two spoons, a pair of holland sheets, and a small table with a green cover.

As the youngest son, Walter Ralegh could expect very little property from his none-too-wealthy father, who was a seller rather than a purchaser of land. In 1561 Walter senior and Katherine created a trust concerning their manors of Bolham near Tiverton and Colaton Raleigh, which were to pass on their deaths to Walter's eldest son, George, and in the event of his dying without heirs (which he did), to Carew and Walter junior respectively. So it was not until after George's death in 1597 that Sir Walter Ralegh enjoyed the possession of the manor of Colaton Raleigh. In 1560, however, the six-year-old Walter was given by his father and eldest half brother a grant for life of £6 13s 4d per annum out of the manor of Withycombe Raleigh, and in the same year Walter senior obtained for himself, Carew, and young Walter a sixty-year lease of the tithes of fish of Sidmouth. They paid a rent of £5 a year to the crown lessees of the manor, and following a dispute in 1562 this was reduced to £3 6s 8d. In 1578 they sold the remainder of the lease to William Periam of Exeter for £60, which suggests that they were not enjoying much profit.

For the second decade of the reign of Queen Elizabeth, neither Devon nor his parents could have seen much of Walter junior. About 1568, at the age of fourteen, he went soldiering in France and the Low Countries with his cousin Henry Champernowne and was fortunate enough to survive what was probably his toughest physical challenge until he went to Guiana in 1595. By 1572 he was at Oxford, possibly supporting himself on what he had saved from his captain's pay. He then moved, apparently without completing his degree, as was the habit of young gentlemen, to the Inns of Court in London.

The year 1578 brought him home to Devon for a while as captain of the *Falcon*, belonging to William Hawkins of Plymouth, one of the ships that sailed from Plymouth in November under the command of Walter's half brother, Sir Humphrey Gilbert, on an abortive colonizing venture to the New World. Ralegh sailed, of course, as a soldier. He and his Portuguese master and pilot, Simon Fernandes, sailed only as far as the Cape Verde Islands, but this was farther from England than was achieved by the rest of the fleet. After this he returned to London, obtained a minor post at court, and in 1580 went to seek his fortune as a soldier in Ireland, the resort of many landless English younger sons and where Humphrey Gilbert had been before him. Ralegh fought the Irish bravely but savagely, and he got pregnant a girl named Alice Gould, possibly a West Country woman. He left her and his daughter (who, many years later, he was to remember in his will) in Ireland, though he is credited with having found Alice a blue-blooded Jersey husband. After this it was London again and entry to the court proper.

By 1583, enjoying the queen's favor, Ralegh was acquiring an income, though more than most of those among whom he moved, he lacked long-term security. His Irish adventures had done no more than whet his appetite for land, and the queen's gift to him of leases of some of the estates of All Souls, Oxford, could easily be withdrawn. So also could his grant of a monopoly of issuing licenses to taverners to sell wine, a favor from which, however, after a false start, Ralegh first made real money. His monopoly of the grant of licenses to export certain cloths was another early profitable venture. What he used as his bachelor's residence at this time is not clear, but in his tavern licenses in 1583 he is described as "of Collyton Raleigh, esquire."[5] It is possible that it was at about this time that he acquired the manor of Hawkerland in the parish of Colaton Raleigh. The manor had once belonged to Dunkeswell Abbey some dozen miles away, north of Honiton, and had been granted by Queen Mary in 1553 to the widowed marchioness of Exeter. Ralegh certainly sold it in 1589 to a Michael Blount, and it later passed to the Duke family, which already owned another former Dunkeswell Abbey manor in the parish.

In July, 1584, not long after seeing Philip Amadas and Arthur Barlowe off on their exploratory voyage to the east coast of North America, Ralegh, now back at court, wrote to one of the Duke family, seeking to purchase Hayes in East Budleigh. It is clear from his letter that although he already owned the small property in Colaton, he desired to own his birthplace:

Mr Duke, I wrote to Mr Prideux to move you for the purchase of Hayes, a farm sometime in my father's possession. I will most willingly give you whatsoever in your conscience you shall deem it worth, and if you shall at any time have occasion to use me you shall find me a thankful friend to you and yours. I have dealt with Mr Sprinte for such things as he hath at Collitone and thereabouts and he hath promised me to depart with the moiety of Otertowne unto you in consideration of Hayes according to the value and you shall not find me an ill neighbour unto you hereafter. I am resolved if I cannot intreat you to build at Colliton, but for the natural disposition I have to that place [Hayes], being born in that house, I had rather seat

This letter was written by Walter Ralegh to Richard Duke on July 26, 1584; it is almost certainly in Ralegh's own hand. Letter held by Devon Record Office; photograph courtesy University of Exeter.

myself there than anywhere else. Thus leaving the matter at large to Mr Sprint I take my leave, resting ready to countervail all your courtesies to the uttermost of my power. Court the xxvi of July 1584.

Your very willing friend in all I shall be able,

W. Ralegh.[6]

Mr. Prideux was probably Edmund Prideaux, esquire, of Netherton in the parish of Farway in east Devon, Walter's contemporary and an Inner Temple man who was a professional lawyer. Mr. Sprinte was Gregory Sprente, husband of Christianne, the only daughter and heiress of Richard Duke (d. 1572) of Otterton. The owner of Hayes in 1584 was the latter's nephew, another Richard, son of Richard Duke's younger brother, John, suggesting that Hayes was entailed in the male line. Ralegh was to be disappointed in his suit, and he even abandoned, if indeed he had been serious, his alternative idea of building a house in Colaton Raleigh. After the sale of his property there in 1589 he never, so far as is known, owned any land in the South West until he obtained possession of his patrimony in Colaton Raleigh in 1597.[7] Even Sherborne he held, from 1592, only as a tenant on a ninety-nine-year lease from the crown.

But the years ahead were to bring Sir Walter, as he became in January, 1585, many links with his native "country," as member of parliament, as chief administrator of the royal Duchy of Cornwall and of the queen's interests in tin mining, as her defense chief for Cornwall and her guardian of the coasts and coastal waters of Devon, and finally as promoter of many of the maritime enterprises for which the seaports of Devon were the base. Legend has it that Ralegh retained his Devonshire accent throughout his life, even cultivating it for the queen's amusement, but the extent to which he identified himself with the people of the South West can be determined only by considering in turn each of his many spheres of activity.

Sand (*top*), in the parish of Sidbury, east Devon, remains very largely as it appeared when it was rebuilt in and after 1594 by Rowland Huyshe, the Puritan eldest son of a London grocer. The mansion is built principally from local flint stones, as Sir Walter Ralegh would have used had he built his mansion in Devon. Poltimore Farm (*bottom*), in the parish of Farway in east Devon, a medieval structure with a later wing, is probably similar to Hayes as it appeared in the mid-sixteenth century. Photographs by the author. Photograph at top courtesy Lieutenant Colonel Patric Huyshe; at bottom courtesy Mr. and Mrs. Huffman.

II. The South West and Its People

The road to the South West that Ralegh knew so well began, and indeed still does, at the bridge over the Thames at Staines in Middlesex. Thence it lay through Hampshire via Basingstoke and Andover to Salisbury in Wiltshire, Shaftesbury, and Sherborne in Dorset, into Somerset at Crewkerne and from there to Honiton in Devon, sixteen miles from Exeter. Only an eccentric traveler such as John Leland, who came to the South West in about 1540, would take the difficult northern coastal route, and those coming from Bristol via Taunton in Somerset would usually proceed to Exeter. Once across the river Exe, except for those with business in north Devon, the obvious route westward was via Ashburton and so to Plymouth. To proceed thence into Cornwall involved a considerable journey inland to cross the river Tamar, which, in the sixteenth century and for nearly three centuries to come, made Cornwall almost an island. The bishops of the great diocese that then covered the whole of Devon and Cornwall rarely visited the latter or indeed felt very inclined to penetrate far beyond their cathedral city of Exeter. Ralegh too seems to have felt that east Devon, or even mid-Dorset, was as far as he wished to remove himself from the metropolis.

Only twenty-five miles or so west of Sherborne the peninsula narrows to a mere thirty-five miles between Bridgwater and Lyme bays. But by the longitude of Exeter the county of Devon widens north to south so that from Foreland Point to Prawle Point, as the crow flies, is a distance of seventy miles. Westward the width narrows again, but Cornwall thrusts itself so far out into the Atlantic approaches that Lands End lies some 120 miles from the Devon/Dorset border, and the Isles of Scilly even farther. Much of the peninsula, especially Devon, is composed of high land more than 400 feet above sea level. Although in the northwest the highest parts of Exmoor (over 1,600 feet) are in Somerset, the foothills extend down to a bare ten miles from Exeter. Even more of Devon is covered by the great granite mass of Dartmoor, and there are four more granite moors in Cornwall, the largest being Bodmin Moor not far from the Devon border. The peninsula is scored by many rivers, not only the Tamar, and the Exe, which

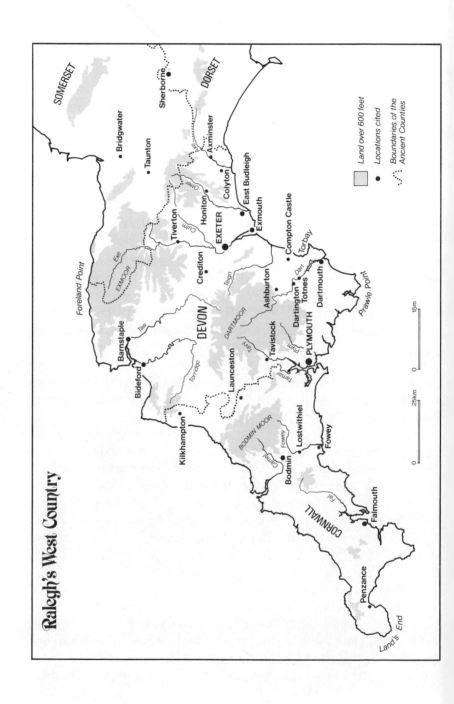

Ralegh's West Country

SOMERSET

DORSET

Sherborne

Bridgwater

Taunton

Axminster

Colyton

East Budleigh

Tiverton

Honiton

EXETER

Exmouth

Compton Castle

Torbay

Crediton

Ashburton

Dartington

Totnes

Dartmouth

DEVON

EXMOOR

DARTMOOR

Tavistock

PLYMOUTH

Prawle Point

Foreland Point

Barnstaple

Bideford

Launceston

BODMIN MOOR

Lostwithiel

Fowey

Kilkhampton

Bodmin

CORNWALL

Falmouth

Penzance

Land's End

Exe
Culm
Otter
Axe
Teign
Taw
Torridge
Dart
Tavy
Plym
Tamar
Fowey
Camel
Fal

Land over 600 feet

Locations cited

Boundaries of the
Ancient Counties

0   15m

0   25km

drains the heights of Exmoor into the English Channel, but also the Taw and Torridge, which flow broadly northward in Devon, and a host of lesser rivers, such as the Otter in east Devon, all of which have produced a deeply indented southern coastline in both counties.

Like Tudor England in general and the highland zone to the north and west in particular, Devon and Cornwall were sparsely populated. Tax assessments that survive for the early sixteenth century show that the greatest concentration of householders of any substance, over twenty per square mile, was in a wide band of country extending from the southern tip of Devon between Dartmoor and the sea as far as the Exe estuary and some way inland into middle and northeast Devon. Much of north Devon, the area due west of Exeter, and the far east of the county contained on average only between ten and twenty taxpayers in each square mile; and there were two areas, one extending from the northwestern fringes of Dartmoor to the Cornish border and the other to the western edge of Exmoor in north Devon, where there were fewer than ten. Dartmoor itself and most of Exmoor were devoid of permanent habitation. Around Plymouth, up the river Tamar, and over into southeast Cornwall the tax assessments indicate more than fifteen taxpayers to the square mile, and farther west they show a greater concentration on the southern coast persisting all the way though becoming less dense toward the western extremity. On the north coast and in the Lizard peninsula there were fewer than ten households to the square mile. The total area of Cornwall was about half that of Devon, but in the early sixteenth century there were fewer than one third of the number of taxpayers. These are crude figures, leaving out of account the poor who paid no tax and also the densely populated city of Exeter, where about 8,000 people were packed within the walls into an area of less than 100 acres, little more than one tenth of a square mile. But they tell a significant tale, namely that people in the southwest peninsula were not very thick on the ground. That said, however, it must be added that Devon and Cornwall were not very different from England as a whole, large parts of which, especially the North and the West Midlands, had barely ten taxpayers per square mile.[8]

Devon, with seventy boroughs, and Cornwall, with thirty, rank among the top three counties in England both in the actual number of boroughs and their density compared with total county acreage, but most of these represented either tenurial eccentricities or frustrated seignorial ambitions. In fact there were in the South West few real towns in the sense of large concentrations of people living in close proximity to their neighbors. Only Exeter and Plymouth numbered their population in thousands, though there was a handful of smaller and well-established towns with a distinctly urban character, notably Barnstaple, Totnes, Tavistock, and Launceston in Devon and Bodmin, Wadebridge, Lostwithiel, and Helston in Cornwall. Far more numerous, especially in Devon, were the country towns, the largest of all being Crediton, only eight miles northwest of Exeter, closely followed by Tiverton, Cullompton, and Ottery St. Mary, all east of the Exe, and, farther east still, Colyton and Axminster.

Population density as indicated by such records as the muster rolls of 1569 can be deceptive. Barnstaple in north Devon, a busy market town with its gates if not its walls still intact, could muster only about 120 able men, not many more than the village (though even at the present time it calls itself a town) of Hartland on the remote northern coast. A reference to a map of parish boundaries, however, shows that what look like heavy concentrations of able men often occur in those places where a country town was at the center of a particularly large parish. Tiverton and its two neighbors, Bampton and Halberton, are good examples, and to some extent this explains the concentration of manpower in Staverton on the Dart and at Paignton on the south coast. One of the largest early Elizabethan musters in Devon was that at Torrington on the river Torridge, where the presenters listed almost five times as many able men as were paraded at the port of Bideford. There were, of course, historic and still compelling reasons why people should live inland rather than on a coast vulnerable to sea raiders. Seaside residences are a very modern, and still overrated, attraction. Most of the people of Devon and Cornwall lived in or within walking distance of small inland villages comprising some thirty to forty households with a total population—men, women, and children—of about 200 or so. East Budleigh, its village center some two miles from the sea but including in the sixteenth century the coastal hamlet of Salterton, mustered in 1569, besides George Ralegh, gentleman, on a horse, 8 archers, 10 gunners, 9 pikemen and 7 billmen, 35 able men in all, indicating a total parish population of about 300. This is above average for the whole county of Devon, and Cornish parish priests probably numbered their flocks, on average, rather less.

In both counties, as in England as a whole, the population in both towns and countryside had been growing in the second quarter of the century, though probably not at a pace that, by the year of Walter Ralegh's birth, had made much impression on contemporaries. Crude calculations for Devon based on less-than-satisfactory sources point to an increase from about 125,000 in the early 1520s to 150,000 in the 1570s, that is, about 20 percent over the half century. The rate of increase in the population of Cornwall may have been even higher still, certainly greater than the 15 percent by which the population of England as a whole is thought to have increased during the same period. Those parish registers of baptisms, marriages, and funerals which have survived for Devon and Cornwall, many from the date of their introduction in 1538, almost invariably show, for most years, an excess of births over deaths and a perceptible increase both in the number of weddings and in the size of families.

The parish registers also show very clearly that the South West was not immune from the devastating visitations of plague and other epidemic diseases, which not only killed so many people but also weakened those who survived, especially those families who lost their breadwinner. Exeter was badly hit by bubonic plague in 1546 and 1547, and Barnstaple in those years lost about one tenth of its population. Crediton, on the main road to north Devon, seems to have suffered particularly badly and frequently from this disease, but the heaviest death toll occurred to the southwest of Exeter, especially in the Teign valley. More-isolated communities were less afflicted by plague. In 1551 sweating sickness was more widespread but less deadly. In 1557-1559 a form of influenza caused the small parish of Broadhembury in east Devon to bury a total of 59 persons, five times its normal rate, and at Colyton, with its larger population, the total for the same three years was 177, half as many again as normal. The 1560s and early 1570s brought some relief, and the population recovered; but there were few years when plague was unknown. Crediton continued to suffer, losing a quarter of its people in 1571 and more than a fifth in 1591-1592. In April, 1578, plague was widespread in Cornwall. The worst year was 1589, when the disease was brought into Plymouth by ships returning from Portugal. The city suffered 448 deaths, about a tenth of its population.[9]

Although the South West did not, like London, experience endemic plague, the increasing resort to its larger ports by returning soldiers and seamen more than made up for its distance from the main national trade routes. At Barnstaple the authorities made great efforts to prevent people suffering from plague from coming in by road, but it is probable that most of the town's afflictions in this respect were seaborne. The result was to put a brake on population growth. Although the size of the towns and larger villages was partly maintained by local migration, the effect of longer-distance migration (which was always toward London and the South East) on the region as a whole was, though only marginal, to deplete rather than augment its population. By the 1580s Richard Hakluyt was saying that England had a surplus population—an argument for promoting colonization—but he was a Londoner, conscious only of the hordes of poor and underemployed men and women who were forever pouring into the metropolis. Even in Elizabethan Exeter, which was growing but only very slowly, he would have told a different tale.

III. Farming and Farmers

It is probably no exaggeration to say that nine out of ten households in Devon, and nearly as many in Cornwall, derived their living primarily from the land. The nature of their farming varied, of course, depending on what their land would produce. In the river valleys, especially on the bloodred soils of the Exe and its tributaries, and on the coastal lowlands, such as those in the South Hams of Devon, farming was mixed as between crops and stock, the animals' manure providing most of the essential fertilizer. These were the areas of densest population. Farms on higher and less densely populated ground, especially those on the lower slopes of Exmoor and Dartmoor, contained less than the minimum amount of arable land (usually put at about 30 acres) needed for subsistence, but their owners or occupiers kept proportionately larger flocks of sheep, grazing them on the moor in summer and bringing them down to lower levels in the autumn for slaughter or breeding. The hill farmers relied on the country markets for much of their grain, and with the sale of their sheep and wool theirs was rather more of a cash economy.

Probate inventories are not available in the same numbers for the South West as for other parts of England and in any case are a poor indication of what men possessed in the prime of their lives, but in the fifty or so that survive for Devon for the period 1550-1620 only about half mention grain, either in the ground or in barns. Wheat and oats, followed by barley and rye, were the crops most frequently "appraised." Edward Chamber of Culmstock in east Devon died in 1592 possessed of 2 acres each of wheat and rye and 6 acres of oats, and he also had wheat, rye, malt, and oats stored in his barns. His stock consisted of 7 cows and a bull, 2 yearling cows and a calf, 36 sheep, a mare, and one pig. He also had a dozen "stocks" of bees whose honey must have been a welcome addition to the family's diet. His grain, valued at £7 10s, and his stock, at £31 10s, accounted for nearly three quarters of his worldly wealth, the rest being his furniture, bedding, clothing, and household utensils. He also possessed a stock of cheese and butter and two sides of bacon.[10]

Most Devon farms were small, and those of Cornwall smaller still, though in both counties many a small acreage of arable land had "appurtenant" to it very extensive grazing rights. There is little evidence in either county in the sixteenth century of the "engrossing" of farms, that is, the appearance of capitalists acquiring large acreages on which to produce considerable quantities of grain for the markets. Such grain was more often supplied by the small surpluses of ordinary husbandmen. Even the "yeoman" farmers, who were quite numerous, especially in Devon, were differentiated more by the security of their tenure than by their economic status. There were few commercial graziers. Not all farmers kept cattle, except for a milking cow or two. In north Devon pairs of oxen, used for plowing and harrowing, were fairly common, but throughout the South West, as Ralegh and his military friends were to bemoan, horses were not widely bred and were only rarely used for plowing. Gentlemen, of course, used horses for riding; but carts and wagons were few, and such goods as were transported were largely manhandled.

Sheep, however, were ubiquitous. In the words of John Hooker, appearing in his "Synopsis Chorographical" of the county of Devon (ca. 1600): "although they be not seen in great flocks as they be in the open countries yet in multitude they be more and greater." Hooker showed his capacity for establishing his scholarly credentials when he volunteered the information that in most parishes the church's tithe of wool was worth between £5 and £20 and in some £100 and more.[11] At current market values, £200 would buy about 4,000 pounds of wool, the clip of about 1,000 sheep; and if that was the average per parish, then Elizabethan Devon had about 450,000 of those four-legged fertilizer machines, rather under four per acre. Devon wool, while inferior to the better Cotswold or Hereford fleeces, was said in 1600 to be, at its best, "better than the Dorsetshire wool by 5d or 6d in the pound." Cornish wool, though improving in quality, was still described somewhat contemptuously as "Cornish hair."

The great majority of the farmhouses of Devon and Cornwall were not located in "nucleated" villages but in small hamlets of up to half a dozen or in complete isolation deep in the countryside in sheltered valley "bottoms." Except for those situated in or near the more ancient villages and country towns, they had all their arable soil and meadowland, and some of their pasture, in enclosed fields. Much land had been enclosed ever since it had first been colonized early in the twelfth century, and a good deal had been enclosed since then—

not by landlords or by the larger farmers, nor for sheep pastures, but by general agreement for each man to use as he pleased. Richard Carew claimed that Cornish farmers had made much progress in this direction in his own lifetime, and he compared Cornish agriculture very favorably with the "mingle-mangle" of open-field strip farming to the east, though he was thinking of farther afield than Devon. The huge hedge banks with which Devon farmers had enclosed their fields were already being criticized as wasteful of land, but they were defended by John Hooker, who pointed out what late twentieth-century farmers are slowly rediscovering, that hedges not only facilitate the movement of stock to new and sweeter pastures but also provide timber, which was in increasingly short supply in

This photograph of the Devon countryside about eight miles north of Exeter (elevation about 500 feet) shows the region's undulating terrain, irregular field patterns, hedges, and scattered farms. Photograph (1983) supplied by the author.

England as a whole. There was still some open-field farming in the South West, mostly adjacent to ancient nucleated villages such as Braunton in north Devon, where vestiges of it are still visible. There each of the dispersed strips occupied by individual farmers had to be tilled, harvested, and made available for the communal grazing of stock in accordance with an agreed routine. As late as 1600 a plaintiff in the Court of Chancery spoke of his land at Sheepwash in the Torridge valley in northwest Devon as lying in scattered strips in two great open fields, but this was atypical.

For a townsman, Hooker wrote appreciatively of his country's farmers, and especially of their technical progress. The poorer soil was being improved in various ways by the digging and spreading of marl (clay); by the burning of turves and spreading of the ashes; and by the application of lime, sea sand, and even seaweed. Cornish farmers too, according to Carew, were learning that barley would grow where wheat would not and that it was quick to ripen in the far west. Hence they were increasingly able to enjoy the taste of English beer in place of their traditional oatmeal ale. Of late, Carew recorded: "the Cornish husbandman conformeth himself with a better supplied civility [life-style] to the eastern pattern which hath directed him a more thriving form of husbandry." One wonders, however, whether Cornishmen believed the tale brought back by Amadas and Barlowe in 1584 that on the eastern seaboard of North America "corn" could be harvested three times a year.

It was, of course, the weather that made or marred the harvest, and if the price of grain in the Exeter market is any guide, 1582, 1583, and 1584 were good years, at least for consumers. In October, 1579, the queen's Privy Council, informed of a grain surplus in Devon, authorized William Curtis, a Londoner, to ship 300 quarters of wheat to Spain or Portugal so that he could return with salt, which the country badly needed. He was to do this "without enhancing of the prices or troubling of the markets." When yields were good, grain was even exported from Cornwall, mostly to Spain, and the official closure of that trade in the late 1580s must have upset all who were unwilling or unable to engage in smuggling or in the victualing of privateers. Hooker in fact particularly mentions the growing needs of shipping for "beefs, barons and porks . . . biscuit and beer and cider, beans and peas," but it is unlikely that the victualing of ships benefited many farmers beyond the immediate hinterland of the seaports. In the 1590s, when there was more maritime activity, the South West suffered with the rest of the country from disastrous harvests. At such times, the people of the seaports survived better than the inland population, especially the hill farmers and their families. In 1597 the authorities at Barnstaple sent no fewer than three ships to Dantzig in the Baltic for supplies of grain, but the townsfolk rarely felt under any obligation to relieve the rural population, whom they always suspected of withholding supplies.

There were those who alleged that official purchases of victuals, and especially the dreaded "purveyance" at the crown's price, actually discouraged increased production and in the long run raised prices. Richard Carew, however, argued that "dearth," in the sense of good prices for the farmer, was possible without scarcity:

There are no two trades which set so many hands on work at all times of the year as that one of tillage. The husbandman finding profit herein is encouraged to bestow pains and charges for enclosing and dressing of waste grounds which therethrough afterwards become also good for pasture. With the ready money gotten by his weekly selling of corn [grain] he setteth the artificer on work, who were better [advised] to buy dear bread, being but part of his meat [food], and which he countervaileth again by raising the price of his ware, than to sit idly knocking his heels against the wall.

Carew went on to argue—against the still-prevalent notion that the marketing of grain, especially if this meant transporting it to other areas, depleted local supplies—that people must take a long view, for "through hope of vent [farmers] hold on [to] their larger tillage."

In fact many of the farmers in this still-underpopulated region could be flexible in the amount of land they tilled, following the ancient Celtic system of cultivating a permanent core of "infield" plus temporary cropping of "outfield" taken in from the waste that they would otherwise use for pasture. Once exhausted, this temporary enclosure could revert to the "furze and heath" that was so often appurtenant to their holdings. True moorland, the "high mountains, barren ground" or the "wild marsh and forest ground," of which John Leland had been so much aware in about 1540, was, of course, fit for little but very rough summer grazing; but there are places, such as the slopes of Hound Tor on southeast Dartmoor, where recent excavation has shown that there had been cultivation and even permanent homesteads in the fourteenth century. Elizabethan Devon still, in fact, had much spare land available and suitable for permanent "new takes." In 1630 crown surveyors reported that there were in the South West thousands of acres of waste, and as late as 1811 there were said to be 150,000 idle acres in Devon capable of being farmed.

Some of the Elizabethan nibbling on the waste was undertaken by poor squatters, but evidence of rural poverty and of complete landlessness in the region is scarce. Most of the new colonization was undertaken by already established farmers adding to their copyholdings or, more likely, taking leases for the typically West Country term of years determinable on lives. A growing population meant more younger sons to be provided for in this way and also more marriage portions for daughters; for in regard to inheritance of the main holding, primogeniture was the rule in the South West for landlords and tenants alike. There was thus little of the fragmentation of farms associated in other parts of the country with divisible inheritance. All of this, not forgetting an enervating climate, bred in Devon's farmers a certain inertia that some would call lack of enterprise, others sheer laziness. Above all, Devon's farmers pleased themselves. Sir Walter Ralegh perhaps recalled his rural boyhood when in faraway Westminster on November 4, 1597, in the course of a debate about a bill for the compulsory sowing of hemp, he told his fellow members of parliament: "I do not like this constraining of men to manure [till] or use their grounds at our wills, but rather let every man use his ground to that which it is most fit for, and therein use his own discretion."[12] Astonishingly for a man so involved in maritime affairs, he went on to say that hawsers, cables, cordage, and the like could be got from abroad. The same session of parliament debated a tillage bill requiring all farmers to plow one third of their land. But some, Ralegh argued, were too poor to buy the seed. And why plow up good pasture? "I think the best course is to set corn at liberty and leave every man free, which is the desire of a true Englishman." For that the Devon farmers might have partly forgiven him for the alleged effect of his cloth export licensing monopoly upon their economy.

John Hooker placed the manufacturer of woolen cloth next in importance to farming among the occupations of his fellow Devonians. He was not thinking only of the small master weavers and cloth finishers of Exeter and all the country towns of Devon—especially Crediton, Tiverton, Cullompton, Honiton, Ottery St. Mary, and Colyton—but of the nonagricultural employment of so many farming families as well. He wrote: "Wheresoever any man doth travel you shall find at the hall door, as they do name the foredoor of the house, he shall I say find the wife, their children and their servants at the turn [wheel] spinning or at their cards carding and by which commodity the common people do live." Edward Chamber of Culmstock who, as already indicated, was a small farmer, had in the house at his death no less than seven pounds of black woolen yarn. Although neither wheels nor looms were listed, he or members of his family must either have spun this yarn themselves—perhaps from their own wool, which they had washed and carded (a process involving pairs of wooden boards set with metal teeth)—or have been preparing to weave a kersey cloth on a narrow Devonshire loom. The latter is more likely, as the yarn had already been dyed.

These early to mid-sixteenth-century bench ends are in East Budleigh church. The bench end at left depicts a ship of the period; the one at right shows an angel above two implements of the woolen cloth industry, a wooden handle set with teasel heads for raising the nap of woven cloth, and a pair of shears for trimming the surface. Photographs by the author.

Hooker explains how these specialists would visit the nearest market week by week to sell the products of their labor and buy new supplies. Their skills were merely an extension of those traditionally applied to the making of homespun cloth for their own use. Collectively they were the backbone of Devon's, and indeed of England's, major manufacturing industry. The cloth they made—not only the lightweight kerseys but also the more durable serges, which replaced kerseys about 1600—were not to be compared in quality with the broadcloths of Gloucestershire and Wiltshire, but after being fulled and also dyed in Exeter or in one of the smaller cloth centers, they found a ready market at home and abroad. With the cash thus provided, many thousands of Devon farmers were able to live in reasonable material comfort, agriculture and cloth-making complementing each other and each serving as some protection against the vicissitudes of the other.

Perhaps because the poor quality of their own wool made the resulting cloth unsalable, Cornish countryfolk spun and wove only for their own use. Carew mentions that in the far West the women and children made rush mats for transport by sea to London, but he lists tin mining as first and foremost among Cornish occupations, even prior to agriculture.

IV. Tin Mining and Tinners

When in 1595 Ralegh wrote of the Cornish that "by reason their riches consisteth in tin works, there is little corn and less of all things else," he knew, of course, that tin mining occupied a large number of Devonians too. In spite of the great granite mass of Dartmoor, however, the industry never dominated Devon's economy to the extent it did that of Cornwall.

Tin in its raw state occurs both in lodes deep down in rock strata and in loose ore washed out and deposited in streams. It was the shoveling and washing of the alluvial tin that largely occupied the tinners of the South West throughout the sixteenth century, although shaft mining had already begun in Cornwall. In 1584 a few Cornishmen were involved in building, in a valley near Neath in South Wales, the first water-powered smelting works—the beginning, it has been claimed, of the Industrial Revolution. Since about 1515 production in Devon had been declining, the tinners continuing to scratch only a bare living from their tin streaming. In Cornwall, and to a lesser extent in Devon, the industry lent importance to the stannary towns, four in each county. These were the places where all tin, after smelting, had to be presented for payment of "coinage," a tax levied by the crown but which formed part of the revenues of the duchy of Cornwall. Because of its very considerable financial interest, the crown, over many centuries, had accorded to everyone concerned with the extracting of tin, whether as owners of tin works or as working tinners, quite extraordinary privileges. These included freedom of access to privately owned land that had not already been "bounded," that is, staked out, by anyone else. Cornish tinners, but not those of Devon, were required to pay to the landowner a royalty on the tin produced. Besides this, all tinners were exempt not only from direct royal taxation but also from the obligation of all men between the ages of sixteen and sixty to muster as part of their county militia. Instead, they did so under their own special leader, the lord warden of the Stannaries. Finally, all tinners enjoyed the privilege of being tried for all offenses, even those unconnected with tin mining, in their own stannary courts. Of minor significance by the sixteenth century was their freedom from any taint of villeinage.

The lord wardenship was an ancient office under the duke of Cornwall, and the holder was usually also high steward of the duchy. As there had been no eldest son of the monarch since the death of Henry VIII, the duchy had reverted to the crown. From Henry Courtenay, marquis of Exeter, who had been executed in 1538, the offices had passed first to John Lord Russell, later first earl of Bedford and, after a lengthy gap following his death in 1555, to Francis, the second earl. The lord wardenship carried great prestige and the opportunity of exercising considerable patronage, for the eight stannaries and their courts employed a hierarchy of officials. In practice all the work was normally done by the two deputy wardens, invariably prominent local knights and gentlemen. In Cornwall Sir Richard Grenville held the office early in Elizabeth's reign but was succeeded in 1584 by William Carnsew of Bokelly, gentleman, himself an owner of tinworks and a great promoter, with the help of foreign engineers, of the new mining technology.

In July, 1585, the second earl of Bedford died, leaving as his heir his thirteen-year-old grandson. Clearly, the vacancy had been anticipated, and the earl's successor was immediately appointed. This was Sir Walter Ralegh, who stepped into the twin offices of lord warden and high steward. With a Spanish invasion now almost a certainty and Devon or Cornwall the likely landing place, the military leadership of what were described as "a multitude, ten or twelve thousand [of] the most strong men of England," was of crucial importance. The same unknown correspondent went on to express to Lord Treasurer Burghley the opinion that, "It were meet their governor were one whom the most part well accounted of, using some familiarity and abiding amongst them." This, so far as Ralegh was concerned, was very near the bone. It was indeed true that he possessed neither "seat" nor lands in the South West; and apart from his very extensive "cousinage," he must have been largely unknown in the tinners' country of west Devon and a complete stranger to Cornishmen. The ancestral home at Fardell would have been useful to him, if indeed he ever even contemplated establishing a household so far west. But, since his father's death, that had belonged to his eldest brother, George. It was later sold to a member of the Hele family. In 1539, when John Lord Russell had been appointed, inter alia, to the wardenship, Henry VIII had made him a considerable landowner, especially in and around the stannary town of Tavistock; but with the prospect of vast expenditure on defense, Queen Elizabeth could hardly afford such generosity. In any case, Ralegh was no longer poor. In point of fact, neither of the Russells had resided very often or for prolonged periods on any of their West Country property and had relied upon their deputies to carry out routine duties. From 1586 Ralegh had as his deputy warden for Cornwall Sir Francis Godolphin, like Carnsew an owner of tinworks, and from 1591 his friend Christopher Harris who, though a Devonian, lived in tin country at Plymstock, east of Plymouth. Ralegh inherited as deputy warden for Devon his cousin, Sir Arthur Bassett of Umberleigh in north Devon. When Bassett died in 1586, Ralegh appointed his older brother, Carew, to the post. It was all very much in the family.

Whether Ralegh profited greatly, or at all, from the lord warden-ship is not known. He would be expected to make what he could of the office and of his involvement in duchy affairs, and no accusa-tions of undue profiteering have come to light. The tinners in his charge were a mixed bag ranging from gentlemen who worked their own land (or, like William Strode of Newnham, registered "bounds" to keep others out) to the thousands of working tinners, some of them self-employed and others mere wage earners. Needless to say, there was a steady infiltration of imposters who were anxious to exploit the tinners' extensive privileges, which even included freedom from toll on the sale of their own goods in the markets of Devon and Corn-wall. In Devon the tinners usually presented their own tin for coinage; and from the rolls in the duchy records it is possible to see what a large number of them there were, even when the industry was in decline. In Cornwall the dealers, mostly strangers from London, got in at an earlier stage. In both counties they naturally paid as little as they could. The crown, or the duke, if one existed, had long claimed the right to preempt the tin at a fixed price but surprisingly had rare-ly exercised it. A grant of the monopoly in 1553 to a Gilbert Brokehouse had been suspended almost immediately on complaint from the tinners. Not until about 1600 was it again exercised, and then by Ralegh himself. In the course of the great parliamentary debate on monopolies in 1601 he stated that, "It pleased Her Majes-ty freely to bestow on me that Privilege and that Patent, being word for word the very same as the Duke's is." The house kept very silent. Ralegh elaborated: when tin was 17 shillings and more a hundredweight, he said, the poor workmen never earned as much as 2 shillings a week. "But since my patent whosoever will work, be tin at what price soever, they have 4s a week truly paid. There is no poor that will work there but may work and have that wages."[13]

Whether Ralegh spoke the truth or not, he soon afterward fell into disgrace on other counts and his patent was withdrawn. In fact not even all the working tinners were wretchedly poor, especially in Devon, where many of them were small-holding farmers who worked on the moor as a secondary occupation. Hooker says they lived on their workings in conditions of great hardship but that they presumably thought them worthwhile. Far more of the Cornish tinners were miners first and farmers second. Carew, who is even more eloquent than Hooker concerning the misery they endured, especially when working underground, as the Devon tinners rarely did, marveled that any gain could induce men to undergo "such pains and peril" and pointed out that "husbandry yieldeth that certain gain in a mediocrity which tin works rather promise than perform in a larger measure." On the whole Carew had little sympathy for men whose "calendar [allowed] them more holidays than are warranted by the Church, our laws or their own profit." Ralegh did manage to entice some Cornish miners to go over and work on his Irish estates, but he was never in a position to promise mineral wealth of any kind in or near Roanoke.

Ralegh can have had little to do with the routine work of the stannary courts, or even with the great gathering at Lostwithiel in 1588, when, presumably under the direction of Godolphin, the Cornish stannary laws were revised. He had to be ready to hear appeals from the courts, but evidence of his involvement comes largely from the very end of the century. In 1600 a gentleman tinner, William Crymes of Buckland Monachorum in west Devon, was in trouble with the corporation of Plymouth for allegedly having diverted water from the city's new leat in order to drive his tin mills. The leat was the water supply in whose construction a large, and probably profitable, part had been played by Sir Francis Drake, only lately deceased. Not for the first time Ralegh was incensed that, contrary to ancient custom, which, he had told Lord Keeper Egerton as recently as 1594, was "not to be contradicted by private censure," the case had been taken to Star Chamber at Westminster. He wrote on this occasion to Sir Robert Cecil protesting that he had inspected the offending mills and claimed that they caused "no hindrance at all to the watercourse." How, he asked, could his "poor tinners" pay Her Majesty's exactions and con-

These ruins of a tin blowing mill, probably dating from the sixteenth century, are located on the river Yealm on the southwestern slopes of Dartmoor at an altitude of 1,150 feet. Photograph (1975) by T. Greeves.

duct themselves in a law-abiding manner, "when others can, by a great purse, or by procuring extraordinary means, diminish to their power . . . the common benefit of the people?" According to evidence brought before Star Chamber, Thomas Drake, Sir Francis's brother and heir, acting on behalf of the corporation of Plymouth, had sent two of his servants to spy on the tinners. These men had been promptly arrested by the bailiff of the Tavistock stannary court and on the orders of Crymes had been thrown across a horse with their legs tied under its belly, and they would have been locked up in the dreaded Lydford prison had they not been rescued by Drake.[14]

Crymes appears to have won the day. The authorities at Plymouth had long argued with the tinners about the latter's alleged pollution of the Dartmoor streams, which flowed into Sutton Harbor. Indeed, the Tory brook that Leland had noted as being "always red by the sand that it runneth on and carrieth from the tin works" today runs white with the waste of Dartmoor's china clay. Ralegh's stock had probably never been as high in Plymouth as that of Sir Francis Drake. It is true that sometime in 1587-1588 the city had presented the lord warden with a silver cup that had cost £12, but during the crises of the 1590s Ralegh had used his authority to insist that his "companies of tinners" should not move to the defense of Plymouth except in the event of an actual invasion by the enemy. But there is no evidence that he had so much as a pied-à-terre in Plymouth; and on one of the few occasions when his presence in the area is on record, he was staying out at Radford in the parish of Plymstock with this deputy for Cornwall, Christopher Harris. It was in fact at Radford that Ralegh and his wife stayed, in semicustody, in July, 1618, before being moved, first to the Drake mansion at Buckland and thence to London and the Tower.

Ralegh had never sought popularity, or like Drake achieved it, but a forecast that under him the tinners would be like a body without a head had not been wholly borne out. He had enjoyed the semblance of authority that the lord wardenship had given him, but even more he had enjoyed the opportunity it gave him of tilting at authority on behalf of those for whom he claimed to speak, be they tinners or seamen. It was perhaps typical of him that as he sailed up the Channel on his last voyage home, he offered to land some of his crew on the coasts of Cornwall or Devon in order that they could lie low "until they be pardoned."

V. Fishermen and Privateers

The fourth of the "commodities" that Hooker, writing about 1600, saw as sustainers of the Devonshire commonwealth was "the navy [men of war] and seafaring, as well for merchandise as for fishing." Hooker wrote of the "many good havens and creeks" and of the coasts being inhabited "with great households and families of sea-faring men." It had not always been so. The era of the late-medieval Hawley family of Dartmouth and of the long sea war, official and unofficial, against the French had virtually come to an end with the early Tudor drive against piracy. The effect on the number of seamen had been predictable. When in the early 1540s John Lord Russell had come looking for ships, and more especially for mariners, he had found, as he reported somewhat wryly, that even the fishing boats were manned by women. Two of Ralegh's relations, Sir George Carew and Roger Grenville, the former as vice admiral of the fleet and the latter as captain of the *Mary Rose*, were among those drowned when the great warship capsized off Portsmouth on July 19, 1545. But it is unlikely that many of the crew of the *Mary Rose* were West Country men. Carew's last known communication was a shout to his brother, Sir Peter, that "he had [on board] the sort of knaves whom he could not rule." Of the 700 men on board only 100 were expert mariners (the rest were soldiers, craftsmen, ordinary seamen, and servants), and these were too disorderly, apparently, to handle the ship efficiently.

All around the long coastline of the two southwestern counties there was a string of what John Leland at about this time had called "fisher towns," tiny villages on or very near the coast, from whose quays men set sail in small craft with their nets. John Norden in the 1590s depicted in St. Austell Bay between Mevagissey and Fowey a group of little boats trailing their seine nets for pilchards. A few larger boats ventured farther out to sea for big catches. Most of the owners of fishing boats and their few crewmen were also, partly if not primarily, farmers. If they caught more fish than they needed, they could earn a little cash by selling the surplus to the "jowtars," or fish dealers, who would carry supplies inland. In 1550, at a time of serious food shortage, the justices of the peace of Cornwall, taking their cue from a recent royal proclamation, insisted that all catches be put up for public sale on the "strand" for at least one hour at an agreed price before the dealers had their chance. Even Plymouth, with its own fishing fleet, had long depended on supplies of pilchards from Cornwall.

Always on the lookout for merchantmen using Devon and Cornwall as their base for cross-Channel trade, Leland had dwelt monotonously on the decay of the harbors. At Ottermouth in east Devon he found the haven "clean barred," though he was told that it had been used by large ships less than a century before, when even Budleigh's Salterton on the west bank had been "a thing of some estimation." Had he passed that way a few years later, he would have learned of the efforts of the Duke family to restore the haven. Farther east Leland noted that the people of Seaton were even then endeavoring, apparently without much success, to clear a pebble ridge and divert the river Axe into a deeper channel. Only rarely did he mention seaports. Even at Barnstaple and Bideford in north Devon he was more impressed by the stone bridges spanning the rivers Taw and Torridge than by the shipping, though he saw ships being built on the latter. All the way along the north coast of Cornwall he found few quays or jetties, many choked harbors, and, at most, drawn up on the shore, a few fishing boats in which, he remarked somewhat scathingly, "in fair weather the inhabitants fish."

Not until Leland reached the Helford River on the south coast did he find a resort for larger vessels. Falmouth he recognized as "a haven very notable and famous and in a manner the most principal of all Britain," and the Carrick Roads seemed to him "a sure harbour for the greatest ships that travel by the ocean," an appraisal echoed many years later by Ralegh. Possibly the gentlemen with whom Leland largely kept company were silent about their own maritime preoccupation, but at Fowey Leland noted ample evidence of the wealth accumulated in past times from piracy. Here too he saw merchant ships, although as late as 1602 Richard Carew was lamenting how few there were in Cornwall. They were present too at Saltash on the Cornish side of the Tamar, but Leland, perhaps mindful of his royal master's interests, was more impressed by the many deepwater creeks he saw running inland from Plymouth Sound and the chain defenses of Sutton Harbor to the east of the town. At Dartmouth he found "good merchantmen" and other shipping in its splendid estuarine harbor, as well as "a fair bulwark made of late," and to seaward twin towers linked by a chain. He noted there too the many creeks up the estuary suitable for shipyards. Proceeding to the Exe estuary, Leland dismissed Exmouth as "a fisher townlet," but upstream at Topsham he found "great trade and road for ships that usith this haven" for lack of access to the quayside at Exeter. He was told of the city's plans to make its river navigable for oceangoing ships.

It was to be more than twenty years before, with the help of a Welsh engineer, the merchants of Exeter completed the first stage of what had to be an artificial waterway, the first pound-lock canal in England. Long before this, however, West Country maritime enterprise in general had received a fillip in a renewal of official encouragement to engage in legalized piracy, that is, privateering. This began with the French war in the mid-1540s. It was a highly organized business in which men entered into partnerships to provide and provision ships. The owners were very largely gentlemen, but there had, of course, to be a share of any profits for masters and crews. Walter Ralegh senior and his sons were in from the start, among their associates being young Gregory Cary of Cockington, vice admiral of Devon. One of Cary's official functions in peacetime was to arrest pirates, but in wartime it was easy to obtain licenses to attack enemy shipping or ships alleged to be carrying enemy goods. In 1549 twenty-one-year-old John Ralegh captured a Spanish ship carrying Flemish goods. This was illegal and landed him in trouble in the High Court of Admiralty, and but for this the deed would have remained unknown. The ship's cargo was largely wine, which Ralegh brought into Exmouth (no longer a mere fishing village), and the local housewives came down to the harbor with pots and emptied the barrels. How many legal prizes the Raleghs captured is impossible to ascertain. In 1557 George Ralegh, the eldest of the sons, in command of the *Katherine Raleigh,* captured off the Scillies a Portuguese ship carrying hides and Irish cloth. John led the boarding party. They returned via Mousehole in Cornwall, where they met with a Yarmouth ship whose crew they bribed with gifts of cloth to keep silent.[15] Three-year-old Walter junior no doubt heard the full story back at Hayes.

By now Walter senior was deputy vice admiral of Devon to John Yonge of Colyton. A year later, as member of parliament for Wareham in Dorset, he was able to avoid arrest and trial before the High Court of Admiralty for more illegal activities. Scottish ships, however, were now fair game because the Scots were in alliance with France, and the Privy Council encouraged the Raleghs "to use the Scots as enemies and to take them and use them as good prize'—and this in spite of the fact that Mary's ministers knew that Ralegh had assisted some of the rebel Wyatt's Devon accomplices to escape by sea to France via Weymouth. But if Ralegh or his sons had their lucky breaks, they presumably also lost a good deal of their investment, for, as already indicated, the family's fortunes do not seem to have been permanently improved.

Like other gentlemen, they no doubt kept on hoping for a truly rich prize, even selling land to embark on new ventures. Their interest in privateering, and even in naked piracy, thus rekindled, the gentlemen hardly looked back, waiting only for the day when they could prey on Spanish ships without any fear of the queen's displeasure. They had little interest in legitimate and humdrum merchandising. To a man like Sir Richard Grenville, the discovery of a route to China would, he hoped, bring him "gold, silver, pearls and spice" and, almost as an afterthought, "wax, tar and tallow," and the chance of a prize at sea was always worth a detour. By the end of the century the place of gentlemen as promoters of and investors in privateering had been very largely taken over by merchants, especially Londoners, but as late as 1596 it was said that there were in Plymouth 500 gentlemen "covered in silver and gold lace," including half a dozen aristocrats. Young gentlemen seized every opportunity of going to sea: for experience, for adventure perhaps, but principally in the hope of a share of the spoils. They could be an embarrassment, for they expected to be treated with due deference—until, that is, Francis Drake the yeoman's son taught those who sailed with him around the world that they must "haul and draw" with the rest of the crew.

Walter Ralegh junior owned his first privateering vessel in 1582. By now he could take his choice of seamen. Whereas between 1560 and 1570 the number of experienced mariners in Devon, that is, men capable of handling a ship, rose from 1,270 to 1,675, by 1582 there were more than 2,000, plus 150 ships' masters. In Cornwall the number of masters rose from 40 in 1570 to 108 in 1582, and the total number of mariners and seamen from 1,162 to 1,810.[16] The increase in population by then was not the only reason. Conditions on board the ships were still appallingly hard, but it was the lure of gold that made them worthwhile. Many years later when he was in the Tower, even Ralegh was to complain of the difficulty of persuading men to go to sea unless they could look forward to prizes. He himself, in fact, enjoyed a reputation among seamen for treating them fairly in this respect. In 1592 his ship the *Roebuck* brought into Dartmouth one of the greatest prizes of all, the Portuguese *Madre de Diós*. Ralegh was in the Tower with Bess. Robert Cecil, sent down to salvage what he could for the queen, met what seemed like the whole county coming away laden with spoils. "My Lord," he reported to his father, "there never was such spoil. . . . Fouler ways, desperater ways nor more obstinate people did I never meet with." Ralegh had to be released, and when he arrived in Dartmouth some 140 men, not all of them his own crew, "came to him with such shouts and joy as I never saw a man more troubled to quiet them in my life. . . . I do vow to you before God [that he] is greater among the mariners than I thought for." As his reward Ralegh received from the queen the return of his own outlay and, what was worth far more, his freedom.

Since John Yonge's time the vice admiralship of Devon—an office created only in the mid-1530s—had been held by various local gentlemen including Ralegh's uncle, Sir Arthur Champernowne of Dartington near Totnes. Sir Arthur had had the pleasure, and no doubt the considerable profit, in December, 1568, of seizing two Spanish ships that had sought the shelter of the Tamar to escape French privateers; the vessels contained 600,000 ducats intended for the duke of Alva in Flanders. But most years brought only the profits from wrecks, and local people probably got to the sites of wrecks first, especially in Cornwall. In fact there was no Cornish vice admiralship as such, the duties belonging to an officer of the duchy, which is why Sir Walter Ralegh was appointed to Devon only. What it profited him is not known, but he had the satisfaction of appointing his friend John Hooker of Exeter as one of the judges of his admiralty court. This was not entirely inappropriate, for in his youth Hooker had studied the civil law upon which the law of the sea was based. It is unlikely that either Ralegh or Hooker was ever called upon to deal with cases of piracy, for during the whole of their term in office England was at war with Spain.

John Hooker, in fact, although as a loyal subject of the queen he could hardly object to her subjects' preying on enemy shipping, especially in the English Channel, probably deplored the effect of any kind of war on legitimate or normal overseas trade. He himself had spent some time in Ireland in the early 1570s with Sir Peter Carew, and he found its unruliness very distasteful; and the parliament in

Dublin of which he was a member for a short while seemed to him akin to a bear house. An orderly society and honest trading was his ideal. He was even to write somewhat scathingly of the Roanoke expeditions in his "Annals." Commenting on Drake's return from his West Indian voyage in 1586 "with great spoils and riches and honour" and of course accompanied by the returning colonists, Hooker contended that this "influenced the country with a desire to adventure unto the seas in hope of like good success [so] that a great number prepared ships, mariners and soldiers and travelled every place at the seas where any profit might be had, some into Indians [sic], some to Wyndganne de Coye [sic], some seeking a way to China by the North Pole and some to find that which was not lost, whereby many were undone and themselves in the end never the better."

Hooker was devoted above all else to his native city of Exeter, to its prosperity, to its amenities, and to its civil government. Exeter had a thriving cloth-finishing industry, but its rulers, Hooker's closest friends, were sober merchants. In Plymouth, ever since the 1530s, the Hawkinses had been seeking out and exploring new trading outlets, and indeed as late as 1569 John Hawkins was still endeavoring to do business with the Spaniards on the other side of the Atlantic. But the merchants of Elizabethan Exeter continued to rely on their established cross-Channel trade, largely with France, the trade on which the city's prosperity had been built in the years around 1500. Hooker even expressed the opinion that England was so well blessed with resources that it could better live without other nations than they without it, but in this his Exeter friends, who imported so many foreign luxuries, would hardly have agreed with him.

Exeter was a tightly knit and structured community, the oligarchic city council requiring that no man might trade within the walls unless he was a freeman. Walter Ralegh senior paid £4, an unusually large amount, for his freedom in 1555. In 1561 the merchants obtained a royal charter constituting themselves the Company of Merchants trading with France. As a body, they had little interest in the New World, even for its commercial possibilities. They did invest a little money in Sir Humphrey Gilbert's ill-fated voyage of 1583, seven individuals contributing £12 10s each, but their only substantial outlay was the £475 they put together in 1586 for the expedition of John Davis and Adrian Gilbert to find a way to China. Sir Walter Ralegh, through his brother Carew, appealed in vain to them for funds in 1585, but he was under a disadvantage in that they objected to his two trading patents and in 1586 charged him with demanding excessive fees for licenses to export cloth. He had at least one friend in Exeter, John Periam, who was one of those proposed in 1588, along with Ralegh himself, Sir Francis Walsingham, and others, as governors of a company for northwestern discovery. Periam was in fact mayor of Exeter in 1587-1588, and as governor of the Merchants' Company the same year he tried hard, but in vain, to drum up its support. Ralegh was never on easy terms with the city of Exeter, and never on its gift list.

Among the occupations of the freemen of land-locked Exeter one would not expect to find fishermen, and by the later sixteenth century even fishmongers were few. In 1588 the city's profits from the fish market were said to be fast diminishing. There is, however, some evidence as early as the 1560s of the import of fish from New-foundland. In 1571 John Periam and another of the city's leading merchants dispatched cargoes of cloth said to be bound for Rochelle and Newfoundland, but it is unlikely that the *Genett* and the *Bartholomew* crossed the Atlantic, for the rigors of which they were probably quite unsuited. Even the people of Plymouth were now lacking pilchards, for their traditional Cornish suppliers were discovering a better market on the Continent while impudently continuing to use their fish cellars at Cawsand on the Cornish side of Plymouth Sound. The situation eventually became serious enough for no less a person than Sir Francis Drake to be appointed by the queen's Privy Council to head a commission of inquiry. But Plymouth, unlike Exeter, now had the men and ships to fetch its own supplies from more distant waters and in so doing to beat the Cornishmen in the continental markets.

The death of Walter Ralegh's half brother, Sir Humphrey Gilbert, on his way home from the New World in 1583 has tended to obscure the beginnings of the West Country interest in the Newfoundland cod fisheries, especially that of Dartmouth. In actual fact, Gilbert's use of the Dart estuary as a point of departure for Newfoundland in 1578 (the occasion when only Walter Ralegh and the *Falcon* got even as far as the Cape Verde Islands) had more to do with its nearness to his home upstream at Greenway than with any real interest in his colonizing enterprise by the merchants and shipowners of Dartmouth. In 1583 Gilbert in effect sailed from Southampton, calling in at Cawsand near Plymouth only for water and victuals. Whether the handful of English fishing vessels he encountered prior to laying formal claim to Newfoundland in that year included any from the West Country is not known, but when in 1584 Ralegh renewed Gilbert's colonizing patent, the three towns named as English staples for the trade that it was hoped would result were London, Dartmouth, and Plymouth. But Ralegh neglected to declare any interest either in Newfoundland or its fish, and the first large "catch" to be brought to Plymouth was the 60,000 quintals of fish seized from some Spaniards in 1585 by Carew Ralegh and his step-cousin, Sir Bernard Drake.

In the later 1580s fishermen from the east coast ports, who were finding Danish restrictions on the Iceland fisheries quite insupportable, were moving to Dartmouth, where they were apparently made welcome. By 1588 when, perforce, the voyages were temporarily halted, several dozen Dartmouth ships were sailing each year to Newfoundland; and although a local regulation forbade anyone to sail before March 1, the Dartmouth vessels usually reached the fishing grounds before any of their rivals. Fishermen from other ports deferred to their leadership. For the first time since the great days of the Hawleys, Dartmouth now reasserted itself as something more than a mere outport of the wealthy cloth town of Totnes ten miles upstream. Fishing, rather than pure trade, was now its life. Even John Davis, a local man who in 1585 began and ended his voyage in search of a Northwest Passage at Dartmouth, could find little practical support locally; and when in 1590 he sailed for a third time, taking with him a local ship, the *Elizabeth,* it was only on the understanding that the vessel would ensure some profit for its owners by fishing.

The dried or salted fish was sold very largely on the Continent, and most of the fish oil brought back to Dartmouth was shipped thence to London, whence came cargoes of miscellaneous ships' stores and household goods. It was fish that brought the new wealth to Dartmouth, especially in the early seventeenth century; this enabled the town to begin the reclamation of large areas of its foreshore. Work on the new quay actually began in 1584. Only with difficulty was it persuaded to maintain its Henrician seaward bulwarks and batteries. Nor were Dartmouth men much concerned with civic ostentation. While Exeter was adding a great portico to its ancient Guildhall, the old Dartmouth guildhall in Higher Street, once the property of the Hawleys, was falling into ruin.[17] Least of all were Dartmouth men likely to be interested in permanent settlement overseas.

By 1593 even Ralegh was describing the Newfoundland fishery as "the stay of the West countries," for by then it was probably employing more ships than the cloth trade or even privateering. Hundreds of ships and thousands of men were regularly engaged in the trans-

Atlantic run. On July 24, 1594, Ralegh wrote from Sherborne to Robert Cecil about the danger to the Newfoundland fleet—"above a hundred sail" being expected at the beginning of August—from three Spanish men-of-war lying off the mouth of the Dart. "If those should be lost," he wrote, "it would be the greatest blow that was given to England." During two weeks in September, 1595, no fewer than fifty ships returned to Plymouth from Newfoundland. At Plymouth, too, a great deal of civic enterprise was concerned with fishing. It was for fishing vessels rather than for men-of-war that the New Quay was commenced in 1572 on land reclaimed from Sutton Pool, and Plymouth waited until 1606 before replacing its medieval guildhall with a new one raised on granite pillars and arches. Plymouth Fort was built reluctantly, and only as a result of supreme efforts by Ferdinand Gorges and others did the town really become interested either in self-defense or overseas colonization. Meanwhile, although by the 1590s there were fewer gentlemen among the promoters of privateering, luck still held for some, not forgetting the queen with her receipt of customs revenue. In 1594-1595 no less than 8,323 hundredweight of prize sugar was recorded as being shipped from Plymouth to London. Although the combined yield of Exeter's customs on cloth exported and wine imported nearly doubled between 1560-1561 and 1594-1595, it was in decline by 1599-1600. Plymouth's yield, on the other hand, though never as great, continued to increase.[18]

Barnstaple, in north Devon, was also yielding a phenomenal income to the queen toward the end of her reign, and this in spite of the loss of her old Spanish trade. Here too the Elizabethan and early Stuart corporation devoted much effort to the improvement of "the Strand." John Hooker described the town at the turn of the century as

the chiefest emporium of that part of the shire and [it] may be counted a little city for it hath all things in it as in a city and . . . is a very large, great and sweet town. The streets are somewhat large and very fair paved in it. There is weekly a market and fair twice the year, namely Our Lady Day and St George's Day, with the franchises and liberties appertaining to the same.

Yet, all was not peaceful trade, for here, on an autumn day in 1590, almost within sound of the hamlet on the north side of the town with which the Raleghs shared their name, as the town clerk, Philip Wyot, laconically recorded in his chronicle,

Arrived the *Prudence* with a prize taken upon the coast of Guinea, having in her four chests of gold to the value of xvi thousand pounds and divers chains of gold with civet [African perfume] and other things of great value. Such a prize as this was never [before] brought into this port. . . .

A few days later yet another prize came to the quay at Barnstaple laden with "chests and baskets of gold [that] weighed CCxx pounds." In 1591 the town again rejoiced, this time over three prizes, one with a cargo of wines. Finally on January 25, 1592, the *Prudence* once again passed safely over Barnstaple Bar, the still-dreaded sandbank, escorting yet another prize, which Wyot reckoned to be worth all of £10,000. The owner of the *Prudence,* Richard Doddridge, was typical of the merchants who had by now taken the lead from the gentlemen, shrewdly combining trade and plunder, often on one and the same voyage, but keeping their options open. Doddridge was a member of the Senegal and Gambia Company, and his prizes were probably Portuguese vessels encountered off the coast of West Africa.[19] The wealth of Barnstaple during, very roughly, the period between the defeat of the Armada and the English Civil War is still in evidence in the many very richly decorated plaster ceilings in what were once merchants' houses. Visitors to the town's Guildhall are still entertained by the mayor in the Doddridge Parlour, a room lined with the fine oak paneling on which the owner of the *Prudence* lavished some of his profits. Was it, perhaps, on domestic comfort rather than on landed property that the Elizabethan merchants spent their ill-gotten harvest of the oceans? In Devon, though not in Cornwall, they left behind them far more visible signs of their wealth than the gentlemen. Landed wealth leaves few reminders.

VI. Landed Proprietors

John Oxenham and others, when questioned by their Spanish captors as to the objectives of their fellow Englishmen in penetrating the New World, invariably spoke of their great need of land, not so much as occupiers but as proprietors. In England, of course, the common law recognized no absolute ownership of land but only freehold limited by superior tenure, the only absolute owner being the wearer of the crown. Hence, of course, the necessity felt by all explorers to assume possession in the name of the reigning monarch. Was there, in fact, a hunger in the South West for landed proprietorship? Was there a land market? And was it starved of supply?

Not until the sixteenth century was at least one third over was there a sufficient supply of land to create an active market. However hard-pressed they were, landowners contrived to retain their inheritance intact as long as possible, and even the provision of small patrimonies for younger sons and marriage portions for daughters were made by the creation of trusts. Only death without male heirs destroyed a landed family, and marriage to one or more heiresses was one of the few ways of founding or augmenting an estate. Political misfortune was a hazard usually faced only by men of eminence in national life; and even attainders were rarely disastrous, though they did from time to time serve to augment the crown lands and supply the pool from which the monarchy rewarded a favored few. The crown estate in Devon had not been extensive, but in Cornwall the duchy, traditionally bestowed on the heir to the throne, if there was one, held some fifty or so units, which were mostly manors but which also included a few ancient boroughs. Duchy property in Devon included the Forest of Dartmoor; the manor and borough of Bradninch, near Exeter, to which was attached Rougemont Castle within the city walls; Sutton Pool, the main harbor of Plymouth and the river Dart. Much of the income consisted of nominal fixed rents; and on the seventeen really ancient manors even the customary tenants enjoyed a secure tenancy, which Richard Carew, still smarting from the leasehold threat in 1594, described in 1602 as "a kind of inheritable estate." Manor courts were held every seven years merely to record tenants' names and extract "knowledge money." Even on the thirteen Cornish manors annexed to the duchy following the attainder of the marquess of Exeter in 1538, there were 156 freeholdings and 145 copyholds; and on the fifteen transferred from the Cornish priories of Tywardreath and Launceston there were about 250 freeholdings and 85 other tenancies.[20] The worst that could be said by its tenants of the crown as landlord in the South West was that it drained money (including the "coinage" for tin) out of the region, but among landowners there was the frustration that the property of the duchy, though occasionally augmented, was never depleted, either by gift or sale.

In other respects, however, the crown acted as a catalyst, acquiring from about 1536 onward the extensive landed endowments of the monasteries and chantries, a large proportion of which were disposed of by 1558, some by gift but mostly by sale, very largely to laymen. A land market, so long absent, was created within the decade 1536-1545, as those who could afford to bought, and those without ready cash sold land in order to buy and thus at least to rationalize their ancestral holdings. The crown was also the procurer of the plundering of the estates of the bishopric of Exeter in both Devon and Cornwall. Bishop John Voysey (1519-1551 and 1553-1555) lived to see, from about 1540, over half his property surrendered to laymen at the crown's behest and the revenue from most of the remainder frozen by the grant of long leases. By comparison, the losses sustained by the dean and chapter of Exeter Cathedral, largely in the reign of Edward VI, were not so permanent, but the effect of long leases on revenue in an age of inflation was considerable and the advantage to the lay lessees correspondingly great.

The last decade of Henry VIII's reign had seen one great West Country noble house destroyed and another take its place, though not with the same lands. For well over two centuries ending in 1538, with short intervals, the Courtenays, earls of Devon, had been by far the largest lay landowning family in the South West and hence not only wealthy but politically powerful in terms of tenants and retainers. The execution of Henry Courtenay, first and only Tudor marquess of Exeter, not so much for his overt opposition to the breach with Rome as because of his own nearness to the throne (he was first cousin to Henry VIII) and his wife's affinity with Katherine of Aragon and her supporters, had left a gap in the power structure of the South West. This gap had been rapidly filled by the raising of Sir John Russell, son of a minor Dorset landowner, first to the baronage (he became John Lord Russell in 1539) and in 1550 to the earldom of Bedford, and by the grant to him of very extensive estates. These were largely though not entirely the former property of Tavistock Abbey and were nearly all in Devon. Russell was later granted another landed empire, largely in Bedfordshire. The Courtenay estates were dispersed, mostly by sale.

John Russell was fortunate in that, although himself a relative parvenu, he had no real rivals in the South West. There were no other noblemen with anything approaching his landed resources there, or indeed with their principal estates in the region. John Bourchier, Lord Fitzwarren, who succeeded his father, the first earl of Bath, in 1539 did own what Leland described as "a right goodly manor and place" at Tawstock, about a mile from Barnstaple, and another farther east at Bampton; but his land was largely upcountry, and for the rest of his life he was rarely if ever in Tawstock. The only other nobleman with inherited lands in the South West was Henry Grey, marquess of Dorset as a young man in the 1530s and after 1551 also duke of Suffolk. Half cousin of the young king, Edward VI, Grey owned property in east Devon but maintained no household there. His only political importance was as father of the unfortunate Lady Jane Grey. As Ralegh is said to have remarked, the South West contained no one whom the queen could call cousin.

What the South West lacked in nobility it made up for in knights, esquires, and plain gentlemen, especially the last. Colonization of the land had been late, and in the twelfth and thirteenth centuries many a family had been induced to settle, especially in the more remote and less hospitable parts of the region, only by the grant of a freeholding with a fixed or even nominal rent. Establishing themselves first in the place to which they gave, or from which they took, their names, many of these freeholders had hardly moved economically, but security and lineage had made them akin to, if they did not actually call themselves, gentlemen. Some acquired more land over many generations, usually by a fortunate marriage, and there were those who had "hung up their hats," that is, moved onto their wives' property. Geoffrey Gilbert did just that when early in the fourteenth century he married Joan, one of the heiresses of William Compton of the parish of Marldon. Sir John and Walter Ralegh's other Gilbert half brothers were their direct descendants. Many families had sprouted lesser branches that in time had outstripped the senior lines.

Over the years one or other of these would often fail and the property be united. John Acland of Acland, a small estate in the parish of Landkey in north Devon, died in 1553 leaving two sons. The elder, Hugh, inherited intact an estate built up, largely by marriage, over many generations. Hugh himself had married an heiress, Margaret Monk. Hugh's mother was the daughter of a London lawyer, and it was perhaps she who galvanized her younger son, another John, into establishing himself at Culm John in Broadclyst, a former Courtenay property. How he found the cash is not known, but he married a widow, Elizabeth, née Rolle, and there may have been a substantial dowry. After the death of his first wife John married another, and this time certainly a wealthy, widow; but having no heirs he founded no new line, and at his death in 1620 his property passed intact to his elder brother and thence to his great nephew. Thus did the Aclands move near to Exeter, where they still are, not actually at Culm John but in the same parish.

Out of some three to four hundred gentry families in Elizabethan Devon, and perhaps half as many in Cornwall, owning among them well over half the land in the two counties, perhaps half enjoyed the right to bear arms, or at least succeeded in having their claims approved by the queen's heralds. This entitled the head of the family, and often the heads of several branches, to the legal "addition" of "esquire," or *armigerus* in Latin documents. Not all esquires were even lords of manors, but the ability, especially in a national emergency, to call on the active service of their tenants added considerably to their personal status. A select few of the esquires in every generation were knights. Knighthood was not yet hereditary, but apart from those created on the field of battle (never really approved of by Queen Elizabeth) it was usually conferred, by the queen personally, on a dozen or so of the leading landowners of each county, those thought best fitted to serve her either locally or in wider spheres. On the whole the knights of Elizabethan England were a meritocracy, and the three sons of Katherine Champernowne—Sir John and Sir Humphrey Gilbert and Sir Walter Ralegh—were almost certainly without parallel. Yet, not one was a truly substantial landowner. Compton Castle was actually a freeholding of the large former episcopal manor of Paignton, which was acquired in 1557 by the Wiltshire-based Herberts, earls of Pembroke.

Because the crown, especially in the person of Henry VIII, had sold monastic property only when cash was urgently needed, selling prices

42

had been reasonably stiff. Gifts and concessions had been few. By 1558 the greater part of the property in Devon and Cornwall that had left crown hands had been acquired, directly or indirectly, by local landowners, mostly gentlemen, a pattern that continued until the end of the century and beyond. Even the absentee intruders sold out sooner or later, the Wriothesleys, earls of Southampton, doing so in order to concentrate on their estates in Hampshire. Of the larger grantees, virtually only the Lords Petre, whose family roots were in Devon, continued to draw their rents to support their great household in Essex. Outsiders who did settle down, sooner or later, included William Abbot, who in 1546, when he was Henry VIII's sergeant of the cellar, had bought Hartland Abbey in the far northwest of Devon. About 1566 he married the already thrice-widowed Agnes, née Amadas, of Plymouth, great aunt of Ralegh's trusted Captain Philip. The Mr. Crymes of Buckland Monachorum in whose battles with Plymouth corporation Ralegh intervened was a descendant of Richard Crymes, a London haberdasher who had bought the manor, rectory, and patronage of the vicarage, also way back in 1546. Richard Crymes would no doubt have taken the abbey site as well had it not already been granted, on unusually generous terms, to the elder Sir Richard Grenville. Only at the present time, nearly 450 years later, have parts of the manor been reunited with the abbey site on the initiative of the National Trust.

Had he been able to afford it, Grenville would no doubt have bought the manor too; but few of the gentlemen, even those in royal service, as he was, could put their hands on large sums of ready cash. All kinds of ways and means had to be contrived. For example, John Champernowne, son and heir presumptive of Sir Philip of Modbury (who, had he lived, would have been Walter Ralegh's maternal uncle), acquired in 1536, immediately after the departure of the monks, the site of Totnes Priory. Champernowne could afford only a twenty-one-year crown lease, but he no doubt had an eye to eventual purchase. After his death (while campaigning abroad with Peter Carew), his widow, Katherine, entered into partnership with two merchants—John Ridgway of Newton Abbot and Walter Smyth of Totnes—and for about £300 they bought from the crown not only the priory site but also more than 100 acres of grazing land just outside the town. Katherine later released the town property and retained the land as her share. In 1545, on his grandfather's death, her seven-year-old son, Henry, with whom Walter Ralegh was later to go soldiering in France, inherited three manors valued at about £250 a year, to which the grazing land, valued at £14-odd for the grant to his mother, was a useful, if hardly substantial, addition. It was at least likely to appreciate in value more rapidly than the manors.

But it was Katherine Champernowne's brother-in-law, Arthur Champernowne, whom Ralegh was later to know so well, who found the means seriously to play the mid-Tudor land market. Arthur's father left him a small freeholding in the parish of Ugborough, the family's tinworks, and some leasehold property. His first purchase was the former Plympton Priory manor of Maristow near Plymouth, valued for the sale at just over £10 a year. His next step, while still in his early twenties, was to marry Mary, widow of his cousin, Sir George Carew of the *Mary Rose*. As Sir George had been his father's heir, Mary must have enjoyed a substantial widow's portion, and before Sir George's death they had been granted, at a very low rent, a joint life interest in Polsloe Priory near Exeter. Arthur now sold Maristow—first the valuable timber and then the manor itself—and this enabled him to buy Polsloe outright at a small valuation based on the rent the Carews had been paying. He survived his involvement in Wyatt's Rebellion through the good offices of that same John Ridgway, now a justice of the peace, with whom his sister-in-law had done business, and in the same year (he did not even go into exile) he sold part of the Polsloe property, possibly the price of his survival. But in 1559 he exchanged the remainder of the priory site with John Aylworth—a local officer of the court of Augmentations, which had been created in 1536 to administer the new crown property—for the much more splendid though greatly decayed mansion of Dartington, near Totnes, a former Courtenay property.[21] There he had a very convenient base from which to embark in 1564 on duties as vice admiral of Devon that were probably every bit as remunerative as his real property dealings. Arthur was undoubtedly a shrewd man of business who, with very little initial capital, ended up with a fine and compact estate.

Finally, among the minor landowners of Devon who were enabled, by the availability of former monastic lands, greatly to augment their patrimonies, mention must be made again of the Duke family of Otterton. Richard Duke's family had long combined a small landed interest in east Devon with trade in Exeter. Being a younger son, Richard became a lawyer and entered the service of Henry VIII as the first clerk to the court of Augmentations. He wasted no time and had already bought the manors of East Budleigh, Otterton, Doddington,

This watercolor drawing of Dartington Hall, near Totnes, south Devon, was rendered by T. Bonner in the late eighteenth century, prior to the structure's modern restoration. Photograph courtesy University of Exeter; reproduced courtesy Devon Record Office.

and West Budleigh, and had acquired the patronage of the vicarage of East Budleigh for £30, before acquiring in 1544 the family manor of Hayes from his cousin, George. He finally added the manor of Colaton Abbot in 1546, retiring the following year and being included in the Commission of the Peace at the same time as his tenant, Walter Ralegh senior. Although he was a crown official, he had paid the full market price for all his acquisitions. The 1540s offered the best opportunities, but thereafter the land market was always an active one and even received a new lease of life toward the end of the century when a good deal of aristocratic land became available for gentlemen who could find or borrow the necessary cash.

It was, therefore, more in a spirit of adventure and, of course, in the hope of royal bounty that so many West Country gentlemen sought land in Ireland. There is, indeed, some coincidence between those gentlemen who went to Ireland and those who had sold even parts of their inherited estates to invest the proceeds in maritime adventures. The contrast between the gentlemen privateers and their economically more successful successors, the merchants, has already been pointed out. Equally instructive is the contrast between one of the gentlemen most active in Ireland, Sir Richard Grenville, and the former mariner, Francis Drake. Whereas Grenville was desperate enough in 1579 to mortgage, and never to redeem, his grandfather's very advantageous purchase of Buckland Abbey, Drake was able not only to buy Buckland out of the profits of his circumnavigation but also to proceed to invest heavily in house property in Plymouth itself.[22]

Another who tried hard to recover his fortunes in Ireland was Sir Peter Carew. His father, Sir William, at his death in 1537, had owned, besides his mansion of Mohun's Ottery in the parish of Luppit in east Devon, the nearby manors of Monkton and Farringdon; the manor of Mamhead and half that of Shillingford, west of the Exe estuary; property in and near Dartmouth; at Weston Peverel near Plymouth; at Ashwater and Luffincott on the northeast borders of Devon; and land at Georgeham, Lobb, and Churchill in the north of the country and at Witheridge in mid-Devon. According to a valuation made when Peter Carew fled the country in 1554, all this was worth only about £300 a year, though his elder brother, Sir George, had mortgaged Farringdon in 1540 for £140. Sir Peter had begun well by marrying a Lincolnshire heiress, though he had both a widowed mother and a widowed sister-in-law (Mary Champernowne) with claims on his estate. It must have irked him to see his cousin, Arthur Champernowne, enjoying the proceeds of some of his inheritance, especially the quite valuable manor of Stoke Fleming and other property in and near the port of Dartmouth. Sir Peter was already borrowing heavily when he was well rewarded for his part in crushing the rebellion of 1549, but he no doubt lost as much if not more in the 1554 debacle. His heaviest outright sales were in the early 1560s, to the despair of Thomas Southcott, the lawyer husband of Thomasine, his niece and heiress presumptive. Southcott paid Sir Peter £2,000 in July, 1563, for a reversionary interest in what remained.[23] In 1568, accompanied by his faithful friend, John Hooker of Exeter, Sir Peter went off to Ireland, according to Hooker in order to reclaim some legendary ancestral estates in that disturbed country. There, a few years later, he was murdered, a typically violent end to a somewhat turbulent and irresponsible career.

Carew, of course, had had advantages not always given to younger sons. Not so those other Irish adventurers, Sir Humphrey Gilbert and Walter Ralegh. The latter's great chances came during and after 1588, when the plantation of the Irish province of Munster went ahead on lines already suggested in 1586 by Grenville, who, incidentally,

46

claimed that his main aim in Ireland was to carve out an estate for his younger son. By May, 1589, Grenville had sent to Ireland nearly 110 adult male settlers for his newly acquired estates, and Ralegh had sent 144, in all more than 1,000 (not including women and children), a great many more than had gone to Roanoke.[24] To dip one's fingers in Irish land required spirit rather than cash. Estates nearer home were available, but they cost money.

VII. The Defense of the Realm

John Lord Russell's function as president of the short-lived Council of the West (1539-1540) had been largely military, to ginger up local leaders in refurbishing or, where necessary, building from scratch the South West's coastal defense works. The judicial facilities were partly a bribe to men of good will and partly a demonstration of royal power. For the few months that the council operated, considerable sums of money were even made available, both from the former monastic lands and from the duchy of Cornwall, for its members' expenses. Although he was a virtual stranger in their midst, Russell won the respect of local gentlemen and could feel assured of their loyalty. Thereafter, although he had a local residence, the former Black Friary in Exeter, his principal duties lay in London, first as lord admiral, then (after 1542) as lord privy seal and later as a somewhat unwilling commander of part of Henry VIII's army in France. Although rarely in the South West, Russell continued to hold a watching brief there; and should any emergency arise he could expect to be sent down in person.

Russell's first and only real crisis came in 1549 with the so-called Prayer Book Rebellion. Few gentlemen in Devon or Cornwall joined the rebels in the siege of Exeter but, largely on account of their mistrust of Protector Somerset, uncle of the young king, Edward VI, a mistrust that Russell shared, they did not rally with their neighbors and tenants to Somerset's support. Without them, Russell had no local militia. His commission of array was useless. He does not seem to have attempted, as lord warden of the Stannaries, to muster the tinners, many of whom, especially from Cornwall, were probably among the rebels. The siege was lifted with the help of German mercenaries and Lord Herbert's men from Wales. Under Northumberland, Russell's role was formalized with his designation as lord lieutenant of the counties of Devon, Somerset, Dorset, and Cornwall. Russell was angry with his erstwhile friends, the gentlemen. To the city of Exeter, which alone had loyally withstood the siege in spite of some sympathy with the rebels, Russell now became a good friend, obtaining for it an extension of its boundaries and other tokens of royal favor. At first in Mary Tudor's reign the lord lieutenancy lapsed. Bedford, now an old man (he died at the age of seventy in 1555), played no active part in frustrating Wyatt's plan to raise rebellion in Devon, but his acceptance of the Spanish marriage—the cause rather than the result of a pension of 1,000 crowns bestowed on him by the imperial ambassador—must have helped to reconcile people in the South West to the queen, at least in her early years. Most of the older gentry, if not actively loyal, were disinclined to rock the boat, provided their newly acquired estates were not at risk. Those who went abroad, especially to Italy, were mostly young men.

Queen Elizabeth would have preferred to have dropped the provincial lord lieutenancies. She certainly had no intention of creating an hereditary office, but Francis Russell, the second earl of Bedford, now back from his prudent voluntary exile on the Continent during Mary's reign, was the obvious choice to wear his father's mantle. He was appointed in 1559 to the dual lord lieutenancy of Devon and Cornwall, with the city of Exeter, but not until 1572 to the lord wardenship of the Stanneries. Indeed, in 1576 he was also made lord lieutenant of the counties of Northumberland and Westmorland and of the bishopric of Durham. Meanwhile, of course, the counties continued to be administered for civil and judicial purposes by the justices of the peace, their number continuing to grow as more and more duties were heaped upon them by parliament. There had been barely a score on the active list in Devon in the 1540s, but by the 1590s there were more than fifty. The number in Cornwall had crept up to thirty. Once named to the magistracy, men usually remained on the list until they died. As the number of magistrates increased, so the net was cast more widely among the lesser gentlemen, largely heads of families, most of whom had learned a little law while finishing their education at one of the London inns of court. Devonians in particular espoused the law, both as advocates and litigants. Cecil thought there were too many justices, but with barely eighty scattered, by no means evenly, throughout the 600 or so parishes in the two counties, they were hardly falling over each other.

Closely associated with them in their quarter sessions, and with the professional and itinerant judges at the county assizes, were the sheriffs. They were appointed annually, by the crown for Devon and for Cornwall by the duke or lord warden, to carry out what were largely routine administrative duties, including the supervising of parliamentary elections. That there was still life in the office was demonstrated in 1554, when that experienced local politician Sir Thomas Dennis, in his capacity as sheriff, outmaneuvered Sir Peter Carew and forced him and his friends to flee the country. The office was usually held by members of the older leading landed families, but Richard Duke was "pricked" by the queen in 1563. Few men held the office more than once.

What was now new was the regular appointment, possibly before but certainly from the 1560s, of deputy lieutenants, usually five for Devon (although there was no hard and fast rule) and two for Cornwall. These numbers were later increased, especially for Cornwall. These offices, which were unpaid and expensive of time and energy, especially when there were threats of foreign invasion, were accepted willingly and even sought by the leading gentlemen of the two counties. In Devon they were usually held by Gilberts, Carews, Chichesters, St. Legers, and their like, this again being the role of the heads of families, supported both economically and in the matter of followers by the landed inheritances that they alone enjoyed. Technically a province of the crown, appointments to these offices were almost certainly made by Bedford. The 1560s and 1570s were, on the whole, years of peace, and he and his deputies had little to do. Not until the early 1580s was the die really cast between England and Spain. It was only with the departure of the Spanish ambassador early in 1584 that Queen Elizabeth felt free to support an expedition to the coast of North America with the prospect of using the new colony as a base from which to prey on Spanish shipping. She also knew that sooner or later there would arrive a Spanish fleet intent on smashing the English marauders at their base in the South West of England. Even if the Spaniards failed to attempt a landing in Cornwall or Devon, these counties had to be the springboard for defensive action at sea.

By the early months of 1585, not only was the second earl of Bedford getting old at fifty-eight (he died in July of that year), but he had no son, and his heir was his grandson, Edward, still a young boy. Although the government was forewarned, the plan for his successor evolved slowly. Walter Ralegh, chosen member of parliament for the county of Devon the previous autumn and knighted in January, was at once made lord warden of the Stanneries and high steward of the duchy. Not until later that year was he also made lord lieutenant, but not of both counties, only of Cornwall. The man chosen for Devon was William Bourchier, fourth earl of Bath. In view of Bath's obvious limitations, it can be assumed that it was felt that organizing the military defenses of both counties would place too much power in the hands of one man at a time of impending national crisis and not that the task was too much for Ralegh. Was Ralegh in fact intended to serve as more than a figurehead, the main burden being placed, in Cornwall as in Devon, on the deputy lieutenants, men such as the experienced Sir Richard Grenville and Sir Francis Godolphin? Cecil and the queen well knew that Ralegh's heart and mind were in "Virginia," whither he would have gone himself if she had allowed him. Perhaps, however, the queen and her ministers felt more confidence in the loyalty of Devon than in that of Cornwall, from which, for nearly a century, most of the trouble in the South West had come.

But in dividing responsibility for the southwest peninsula, the government was taking a great risk. The earl of Bath's only claim to the office was his superior status as the only nobleman with a residence in the county of Devon. He may even have been suggested by Bedford himself, and if so this was a nice bit of nepotism, for in 1582 he had married Elizabeth Russell, one of the earl's daughters. His own grandfather, the third earl, a strong supporter of Mary Tudor, had, however, been named as her lord lieutenant of Devon, Cornwall, and Dorset for a brief spell in 1556-1557. He had died in 1561. Brought up in Suffolk, whence he proceeded to study at the University of Cambridge, the fourth earl of Bath was a man of scholarly rather than military bent. He was twenty-eight in 1585, even younger than Ralegh, and barely known in Devon. All his local estates were in the north of the county. Cecil must have been fully aware of his limitations, for he wrote advising him to be guided by his deputies, advice that twenty-five years later the earl sought from Robert Cecil permission to ignore.

There is little on record by which to judge the earl, but he seems to have had none of his Russell inlaws' capacity for winning friends. In the early 1590s he, or rather his agents, were very unpopular with his gentlemen neighbors in north Devon, especially the Chichesters, and his men certainly stirred up trouble in the town of Barnstaple. One of his few friends among the gentry was Hugh Acland of Landkey. In 1592 the earl complained to the Devon justices of "threatening speeches" made against him, and he went so far as to have Hugh Pollard, gentleman, a former sheriff of Devon (whom he described as a "mean" fellow), taken to the Fleet prison in London. He even

A large monument in Tawstock church commemorates the lives of William Bourchier, fourth earl of Bath (d. 1623) and his wife Elizabeth, née Russell. The photograph at top shows a detail of the monument. Shown at bottom are life-size effigies of the earl and his wife. Photographs by the author.

accused George Cary of Cockington in south Devon, at the time one of his deputies and later to be lord deputy of Ireland, of making trouble between him and his wife, who was a somewhat formidable woman. In 1598 he took sides in a religious dispute in Barnstaple

and, as a justice, bound over a Puritan alderman to keep the peace—
"the like," recorded the scandalized town clerk, "was never heard
before." This then was the nobleman with whom Ralegh, the only
Tudor knight to be made a lord lieutenant, had to work as the South
West braced itself to face the expected Spanish Armada.[25]

Ralegh's two deputy lieutenants for Cornwall were Sir Francis
Godolphin and the less experienced Sir William Mohun, but
Godolphin's former colleague, Sir Richard Grenville, seems to have
been given special responsibility for Cornwall's coastal defenses. In
spite of his preoccupation with the colonizing project and the amount
of time he spent in Bideford awaiting permission from the queen to
sail, to say nothing of his actual absence at sea for several months
during the summer in both 1585 and 1586, Grenville appears to have
been the crown's chief agent, and Ralegh's right-hand man, in the
South West. Like most of the gentlemen, he was probably more pro-
fessionally competent on land than at sea.

The story of the South West's defense preparations, not only in the
years 1585-1588 but also in the even greater crises of the 1590s, is
a long one of coastal surveys, the building of fortifications, the muster-
ing of men, and the finding of money. Ralegh was not immediately
on the scene. For one thing, he served the queen elsewhere as a
member, with Grenville, of a national defense committee and as an
inspector of fortifications in other parts of the country. He was in
Plymouth in October, 1585, to meet Grenville and again in September,
1586, to deal with Grenville's prize. On the former occasion he was
actually entertained, at the town's expense, by William Hawkins and
Martin White. These were really private visits, and it is unlikely that
he was yet putting his mind to his new public duties. There was also
a second visit in 1586 to Ireland.

Ralegh was in the South West again in late December, 1587, when
he wrote a highly confidential letter to Lord Burghley from Exeter.
He had found, he said, the deputy lieutenants somewhat divided about
the region's ability to raise and maintain a force of 2,000 foot soldiers
and 200 horsemen. Previous musters had been "very chargeable,"
trade was bad, and the last subsidy had not yet been collected. He
had conferred with Sir John Gilbert, Sir Richard Grenville, and the
earl of Bath, and all three were "zealous both in religion and Her Majesty's service"; but there were others "both infected in religion and
vehemently malcontent." Those he feared most were the more
"temperate" men, the "secret hinderers" of public safety. He men-

tioned no names but in a postscript referred to the refusal by the citizens of Exeter to bear their share. The "county of the city and county of Exeter," as it had called itself since 1537, had always jibbed at contributing to the Devon militia, arguing that it had expense enough in maintaining its own walls and protecting its merchant ships against pirates, but it usually came to heel in the end, especially when admonished by the queen. Ralegh expressed his confidence that in general the deputy lieutenants "in their several divisions will easily induce the inferior sort to whatsoever shall be thought necessary for Her Majesty's safety and their own defense." He concluded his letter by saying that he had written to the deputy lieutenants of Cornwall and that he himself was "ready to repair thither with all diligence to perform the rest of Her Majesty's command." It is unlikely that he did so, especially so near Christmas. There was probably little he could achieve in Cornwall beyond what Grenville had already accomplished.[26] In emergencies Elizabethan England relied not upon offices but upon men.

Enclosed with Ralegh's letter was a schedule indicating how the local army was to be selected. Each of the two county stannaries was to supply 200 men, these to be included in the 1,200 and 600 footmen required from Devon and Cornwall respectively. In like proportion the two counties were to provide 134 and 66 horsemen respectively and the city of Exeter 200 footmen. Eleven officers would serve without pay, but all other ranks were to be provided for, from the sergeant major's 6s 8d a day to the ordinary soldiers's 8d. Of the total cost, just over £2,000, of keeping this force in the field for sixteen days, almost one third covered the supply of ammunition: powder, 10 pounds per man; match, ½ pound per day; and lead, 1 pound per man. Clearly there was no room in Ralegh's calculations for the longbows, pikes, and bills of the village musters. No wonder he wanted the queen to bear half the cost. This, of course, was a select force, but behind it, according to the muster roll of April, 1588, were some 10,000 men in Devon alone, more than 6,000 of them having weapons but only 3,650 trained in their use. The corresponding numbers for Cornwall were more than 5,000, 3,600, and 1,500; and had the Spaniards landed, they would certainly have faced, in either county, a hot reception.[27] The biggest headache for those in charge was that no one knew whether Falmouth or Plymouth would be the enemy's attempted landfall. Grenville's five ships, ready as they were for an Atlantic crossing, must have been among the best-victualed and otherwise seaworthy ships to join Sir Francis Drake at Plymouth. Grenville himself remained on land, and, had the Spaniards landed, he no doubt would have been the man to take charge of the militia of the two counties so that, as instructions from Westminster put it, "there be no straining of courtesy" between (at a guess) Sir Walter Ralegh and the earl of Bath.

As it happened in 1588, the citizen army was not needed. The great Armada passed by, and only the ships of the two counties were called upon to play their part in the dispersing of the Spanish fleet. Ralegh's own *Ark Ralegh* was in hot pursuit. Although he seems to have remained on land until the danger to the South West was over, Ralegh did contrive to catch up with the naval action farther up the channel and to play some part in ensuring that not only were no English ships lost but also that the Spaniards did not burn "so much as one sheepcote of this land."

For over a decade thereafter, while the rest of England suffered as never before the anguish of bad harvests, plague, underemployment, and the decay of trade, the South West, although itself not entirely free of these other problems, also faced the possibility and at times the actual occurrence of raids by enemy shipping. Until his fall from royal favor in 1603, Ralegh, along with the earl of Bath, was officially in charge of the southwestern land defenses, but he was also, beginning in 1587, captain of the guard at court, besides being the owner, from that same year, of extensive estates in the Midlands. After Grenville's tragic death at sea in 1591, Ralegh was still able to rely, at least so far as Cornwall was concerned, on Sir Francis Godolphin. The worst year was probably 1595, the year following the visit of the Cornishmen to Sherborne. Men from four Spanish ships, after being repulsed near Padstow by young John Grenville, managed to land at Mousehole in Cornwall, where they created havoc, and subsequently at Newlyn near Penzance, which latter place they set on fire. Only the approach of some of Sir Francis Drake's ships from Plymouth saved the day. Now, if not before, Ralegh had to make a "miserable journey into Cornwall," and to the eye of a soldier the county's condition, especially its topography, was alarming. As he wrote to the lords of the Queen's Council from Sherborne in November, "There is no part of England so dangerously seated [officered], so thinly manned, so little defenced, and so easily invaded . . . and [it] is withall so narrow that if an enemy possess any of two or three straights [necks of land] neither can those of the west repair eastward nor those of the east westward." An enemy in possession of the five-mile "straight" between Truro and St. Piran would enjoy enough deep water to the west, superior even to that of Plymouth Sound, to contain "the greatest fleet that ever swam." Ralegh went on to point out the difficulty of reinforcing Plymouth, should the need arise. He saw no sense in trying to bring men from Cornwall, which "is but an arm of land which stretcheth itself even to the bosom of the enemy. . . . [It] hath no horse of service, the country poor, few gentlemen and those of mean living, and by reason that their riches consisteth in tin works there is little corn and less of all things else." Rather, he thought, Plymouth should be relieved by the men of Somerset. They would not have to cross rivers like the Tamar that were not easily "fordable," and their county "is very rich and full of horse, as well for carriage as for service, [hath] many wealthy gentlemen and [it] aboundeth in victual."[28] Ralegh clearly knew his southwestern peninsula, and any sensitive Cornish gentleman who may have read his unflattering description would at least have had his umbrage tempered with relief. In 1601 the men of Cornwall chose Ralegh as their senior knight of the shire for parliament.

If the truth be known, Ralegh himself was now, if not hitherto, convinced that the Spaniards should be fought at sea and that coastal fortifications were a waste of money, "worthy of scribes not men of war."

VIII. The South West at Westminster

The government's eyes and ears in the provinces were the assize judges on their twice-yearly circuits and, through them, or more directly, the justices of the peace. But in sixteen of her forty-five years, Queen Elizabeth had the benefit of the presence at Westminster, albeit for only a few weeks at a time, of the members of her parliaments—two for each of the counties and two for each of the twenty-one "boroughs" of Cornwall and the eight in Devon, a representation extraordinarily disproportionate to their respective areas and populations. Many of the Cornish boroughs were either Elizabethan creations or revivals, some of the former (for example, Fowey and East Looe in 1571) promoted by Francis Russell, second earl of Bedford. The last Cornish borough to be enfranchised was Callington, near the Devon border, in 1584, but by then Bedford's influence was waning and the promoters were the marquess of Winchester and Lord Mountjoy.

It is difficult to contemplate the body of men concerned without becoming entangled in the "clientage"—not of the government as a whole, least of all of the queen, but of the individual men of influence who sought not only to obtain a Commons house to their own liking but also to bestow the coveted seats on those they wished to befriend. For most of the borough patrons their own liking was not dissimilar to that of the queen. For all the opportunities that the Devon and Cornwall constituencies seem to have offered to strangers, these numbered barely one in five of those returned, for the exercise of patronage by no means precluded the choice of local men. Among the older boroughs, especially those of Devon, which were most urban in character, there were many that insisted on at least one, if not both, of their members being of their own choosing, if not their own resident burgesses.[29]

The knights of the shire were invariably members of leading local landed families, Cornwall in Queen Elizabeth's first parliament early in 1559 being represented by John Trelawney, esquire, of Menheniot and Richard Chamond, esquire, of Launcells. Devon sent Sir Peter

Carew of Mohun's Ottery in east Devon, lately back from a Marian exile in Italy, and Sir John St. Leger of Annery, in Monkleigh near Bideford. In the parliament that assembled on November 23, 1584, the county members for Cornwall were Sir Richard Grenville of Stowe and Sir William Mohun of Hall and Bocconnoc, and for Devon, Sir William Courtenay and Walter Ralegh junior, esquire. Almost exactly the same age as Ralegh and like him new to parliament, Courtenay soon found himself on a committee set up to consider the confirmation of Ralegh's letters patent for voyages of discovery. Other members of the committee were Grenville, Mohun, and the member for Bossiney in Cornwall, Sir Francis Drake, another virtually new member. Most of the West Country members returned home for the Christmas recess, during the course of which Ralegh was knighted by the queen. His selection for the shire was rather extraordinary. Parliament had not sat since 1581, when the members for Devon had been Sir John St. Leger and Sir Arthur Bassett, both of whom were still alive but were not reelected by the county. St. Leger actually sat for Tregony in Cornwall. The sheriff in 1584, who acted as returning officer, was Humphrey Speccot, a fairly minor west Devon gentleman of Puritan inclinations. A broad hint from the court may be surmised.

During the first two decades of Elizabeth's reign it is impossible to exaggerate the extent of the second earl of Bedford's parliamentary patronage in both of the southwestern counties. Many of the Cornish parliamentary boroughs were either duchy property, in most cases manorial estates with a handful of "burgesses," or stannary towns, and as steward and warden respectively the earl was well able to exercise decisive influence. Those boroughs over which he had no official control were largely in the pockets of his close friends, men like his fellow exile Henry Killigrew, who himself sat in 1563 for Saltash and in 1571 and 1572 for Truro. Killigrew was abroad in the queen's service for large parts of her reign, but he had two brothers and two nephews who not only sat in Elizabeth's parliaments but also arranged for their friends to occupy other seats.

Although the residence rule was honored in Cornwall more in the breach than in the observance, the burgesses' obedient return of persons nominated by those close to the court did not result in the total exclusion of members of local families. Many of the professional lawyers who sat for Cornish boroughs were men of local birth but working in London. Richard Trefusis of Lincolns Inn sat for Camelford in 1584, 1586, and 1589. Indeed, of the sixty-two members of parliament who sat for Devon and Cornwall in 1584, at least thirty-two had local connections of some kind. Young men were not excluded. In 1586 the two members for Liskeard were Jonathan Trelawney, aged seventeen, and Richard Edgcumbe, aged sixteen. The latter's father, Peter, was steward of the borough. Richard sat in six parliaments, each time for a different borough, five of them in Cornwall and one, Totnes (1589), in Devon, a town that his father had represented in 1555 and his uncle in 1563. Others, especially outsiders, moved around in quite extraordinary fashion. John Periam, the Exeter-born lawyer who was also mayor and governor of the Merchants' Company in 1587-1588 as well as being one of Ralegh's friends and financial backers, found his first parliamentary seat at Barnstaple in 1584, his next at Bossiney in Cornwall in 1586, and finally he sat for Exeter in 1589 and 1593. He had an older brother, William, who sat for Plymouth in 1563, but in his case his legal training took him to the top of his profession as justice of common pleas in 1581 and chief baron of the exchequer in 1593.

In Cornwall it was not unknown for boroughs to make blank returns, leaving the names to be inserted by the patrons. In Devon, however, where the boroughs, though fewer, were more lively urban communities, they usually made their own choice. Plymouth no doubt usually consulted John Hawkins, who was himself one of its members in 1571 and 1572, and often chose local gentlemen—Champernownes, Gilberts, and in 1572 Edmund Tremayne from Collacombe in Lamerton near Tavistock. Tremayne was the second of five brothers, all of whom had been Marian exiles, two of them, the twins Andrew and Nicholas, having later died of battle wounds in France. In 1571 Edmund had become clerk of the queen's Privy Council, but on the death of his elder brother the following year he retired to his small Devon estate and, then aged forty-one, married a daughter of Sir John St. Leger. He had already sat in parliament in 1559 for Tavistock as a protégé of the earl of Bedford. He was to be a very good friend to Drake when in 1580 he was entrusted by the queen with the great seaman's treasure. Dartmouth began the new reign by obliging Bedford but latterly was more inclined, no doubt in the interests of its newfound prosperity, to return its own merchants. So too did Totnes. Barnstaple, as the only parliamentary borough in north Devon, was under some pressure from its neighboring gentry, but it had a long tradition of independence. In 1559 the town returned Sir John Chichester, another of those who had hurried back from exile in Italy to his house in nearby Shirwell, but his fellow member of parliament was a local merchant, John Dart. Chichester had actually bought the former monastic lordship of Barnstaple, and in 1566 he sold much of his interest to the newly chartered corporation but reserved to his family the nomination of one burgess, who would serve without wages. Toward the end of the century, however, in contrast to the situation at Dartmouth, Barnstaple had on occasion to give the choice of its second member to its other neighbor, the unpopular earl of Bath.

It was no doubt largely the ability of the city of Exeter to pay wages to its members of parliament that safeguarded its independence, its choice usually falling on a local lawyer and one of its merchants. The city owed a good deal to the first earl of Bedford, and one of its members in 1555 and again in 1559 was Sir John Pollard of Forde Abbey, who had been the earl's ward; but in 1562 the people of Exeter refused the earl's first nomination but did elect another of his affinity, Thomas Williams, of Stowford in Harford on the southern slopes of Dartmoor. A local attorney and lately feodary of Devon and Cornwall and already an experienced member, Williams became Speaker of the House of Commons in 1563. Although describing himself in his oration as one "chosen from the plough to a place of estimation," he possessed sufficient courage to beg the queen to marry and provide an heir to the throne. He also knew what Exeter expected of him and ensured that no fewer than five of the city's proposed measures were passed. His reward was a gift of £20 and the doubling of his retainer as one of the city's legal counsel. Some verse on his tomb in the moorstone church at Harford ends with the lines

> In peace of justice where as he did serve
> And now in heaven with mighty Jove doth reign.

Not courtly poetry, perhaps, but there can be no doubt of the conviction that he was one of God's elect.

When the second earl of Bedford died in 1585 leaving no adult heir, a vast network of patronage, parliamentary and otherwise, was almost bound to fall apart. A good deal of his borough patronage, especially in Cornwall, was somehow acquired by the Cecils—William Lord Burghley and his younger son, Sir Robert. The Russell estate fell temporarily into the hands of young Edward's guardian, Ambrose Dudley, earl of Warwick, and Dudley certainly exercised some influence on the choice for parliament. Land ownership was the paramount consideration, of course, but it could be expected that Sir Walter Ralegh as the senior official both of the duchy and of the Stanneries would inherit some influence. Ralegh had so many connections, both at court and in the South West, that he may have pulled strings almost anywhere. Evidence is meager. It is hard to believe that he did not exert himself to introduce into the Commons men who could be relied upon to support his colonizing and other enterprises. As already indicated, he was very active in parliament, both as a member of committees and as a speaker. The Commons, however, always included a great many of his West Country relations and friends. In 1601 he wrote to Sir John Gilbert, his half brother: "I pray you get some burgesses if you can and desire Christopher Harris to write in my name for as many as he can procure."

Harris was a close friend over many years, and he himself sat once for Plymouth in 1584, though never again. After Gilbert's death in 1596 Ralegh made him his deputy vice admiral for Devon. Another of his West Country friends and near-contemporaries was Arthur Gorges, who sat for Camelford in 1589; but Gorges was also a friend of Robert Cecil, and it was more likely Cecil who in 1593 obtained for Gorges one of the Dorset county seats. Ralegh himself sat again for Devon in 1586, and his fellow member was a promising young man of twenty-two, John Chudleigh, born a younger son of the old and often-knighted family of Ashton. John's father had been a Marian exile, and he himself was a ward of Bedford. He had succeeded his deceased and childless elder brother in 1571. In 1583 he had sailed with Sir Humphrey Gilbert, but six years later, still only twenty-five, he died at sea, reputedly while leading an expedition through the Straits of Magellan. His estates had to be sold to pay his debts.

Another close associate of Ralegh was a man of very different mold. This was John Glanville, son of a Tavistock merchant, who became a professional lawyer and rose to be justice of the court of common pleas in 1598. Ralegh had employed Glanville on stannery business in 1592. Glanville had served the Russells and was elected a member of parliament for Launceston in 1584. In 1586 he sat for Tavistock and in 1593 for St. German's, just across the border in Cornwall. In 1600, at the fairly advanced age of fifty-eight, he fell from his horse and broke his neck. His widow, Alice, then married Sir Francis Godolphin, one of Ralegh's earliest deputy lieutenants and since 1586 his receiver general of the duchy of Cornwall. It is pleasant to think of this energetic Cornishman finding happiness again when well into his sixties and of his second wife living to bury him in the Godolphin family church at Breage, three miles from Helston.

But Ralegh was not always a good judge of men. In 1587 he and his brother, Carew, with the London merchant and financier William Sanderson, who married Ralegh's niece, borrowed £600 from a rascally Londoner named William Gardiner, a man who even quarreled with William Shakespeare. It must have been in connection with this debt that Gardiner was "elected" to represent the stannery towns of Lostwithiel in 1589 and Helston in 1593. Then there was Ralegh's solicitor, John Shelbury, a London lawyer who was installed, at very short notice, as member for West Looe in Cornwall in 1593. He was one of those appointed by Ralegh in 1596 to administer his wine patent, and he was able to retain it after Ralegh's disgrace in 1603. In fact, he recovered some outstanding arrears and seems to have been very loyal to his master and to Bess; but as the family's lawyer he was not very clever in safeguarding the possession of Sherborne. Finally there was Edward Hancock. He was a native of north Devon, having come from Combe Martin, where Adrian Gilbert was so successful in exploiting the silver mines. He went to Cambridge and thence to the Inner Temple and married a Bampfield of Poltimore near Exeter. In 1590 Ralegh bought for him for £90 from Justice Manwood the clerkship of the Western Assize Circuit. From then on he was Ralegh's trusted servant and custodian of his seal. Ralegh may

This squirrel sejant spoon (*left*) was probably made in Exeter about 1580 by John Edes from silver mined at Combe Martin in north Devon. The reverse of the bowl features the arms of Sir Adrian Gilbert, Sir Walter Ralegh's half brother, who was extensively involved in these mines. Shown at right is an early Elizabethan silver communion cup made by Richard Hilliard, a goldsmith of Exeter, for the parish of Brampford Speke in Devon. Spoon and cup from the collection of the Royal Albert Memorial Museum, Exeter.

have got him his first parliamentary seat, at Aldborough in Yorkshire, in 1593. In 1597 Hancock became a member of parliament for Plympton in Devon, which was in the gift of Ralegh's friend and the local landowner, Sir William Strode, but Hancock's nomination for Barnstaple in 1601 seems to have come from the earl of Bath. After his election, he sent the mayor of Barnstaple a gift of venison. Prior to this he had been to Guiana with his patron, and so great was his devotion that after Ralegh's execution he committed suicide.

Ralegh's own parliamentary career continued its extraordinary course. After twice representing the county of Devon, he missed the short 1589 session, having been in Ireland in 1588 when the elections were held. In 1593 he was returned for the small Cornish borough of Mitchell, which had fallen into the hands of the Arundell family of Trerice when the Arundells of Lanherne remained Catholic recusants. The next parliament in 1597 saw him as one of the members for Dorset, and in 1601 he sat for Cornwall, the only member of Elizabeth's parliaments to sit for three different counties.

IX. Unity and Dissent

Just as there were no political parties in the Elizabethan scheme of things, so there were no religious sects—only in both cases those who kept in step with the powers that be and those who did not. The queen disliked extremists of any kind, and there were historic reasons why she should be particularly wary of the South West. There, less than a decade before her accession, a rebellion with decidedly Catholic if not actually popish undertones had appeared to offer the most formidable challenge so far to the royal supremacy. The rebels had called not only for the return of the Latin mass but also for such things as images and the saying of prayers for souls in purgatory. The queen also knew that, besides the young gentlemen, a small but significant number of ordinary town and countryfolk had slipped away to the Continent from the South West during her sister's reign, some of them bound for Geneva. Was there then a likelihood that Devon and Cornwall might, by the meeting of these extremes, turn into a hotbed of religious controversy? In fact, as it happened, nothing could have been further from the truth.

Between the Reformation parliament (1529-1536) and 1549 Devon and Cornwall had, like most of England, taken the religious changes in their stride, not with any great enthusiasm but for the most part making no trouble. Insofar as the so-called Prayer Book Rebellion of 1549 had been aimed at putting the clock back and in particular at challenging the obligation to use the new English Prayer Book, it had been something of a watershed. In fact in Devon much of the protest had been against Protector Somerset's tax on sheep and cloth and in Cornwall against what was seen as an alien, that is, "English," intrusion in a county still very attached to its local saints and to the holy days and pilgrimages associated with them. Hence the processional banners. While the people of the South West had, like so many of their countrymen, mildly welcomed the about-turn of Mary's reign, they were probably more ready for Protestantism at Elizabeth's accession than they had been during the reigns either of Elizabeth's father or brother. While it is indeed true that a considerable number of the younger gentlemen had gone into exile abroad during Mary's reign, for most of them, as for Sir Thomas Wyatt, the real objection was to the Spanish marriage. Some, possibly including the second earl of Bedford, had become more radical in their Protestantism while in exile, but for most of them the task now was to support Elizabeth as the rightful queen and to keep England for the English. It must be admitted, however, that the South West had not as yet been much bothered by foreigners—Spanish or otherwise.

On November 26, 1564, William Alley, bishop of Exeter, replied to a letter from the Privy Council asking him to provide information regarding the justices in his diocese (Devon and Cornwall) and their soundness in religion. Alley had probably been promoted to the see by the earl of Bedford, who had certainly accompanied him to his cathedral in 1560. He reported that he had consulted with certain local gentlemen, namely Sir Peter Carew, Sir John Chichester, Sir John Moore, Thomas Southcott of Shillingford, John Parker of North Molton and John Carew of Bickleigh, gentlemen, a well-chosen cross section, even to the inclusion of John Carew, who was not yet a justice but who, along with a Mr. Edgcumbe and a Mr. Budockshide were suggested by the bishop as reliable recruits. Alley also suggested for Cornwall the names of nine men "godly effected."

Far more interesting, of course, are those he called "disfavourers." There were four of these for Cornwall who were already justices of the peace, all described as "very great" or "extreme" enemies, namely John Bevil, John Polwhele, John Reskymer, and Richard Roscarrock. In Devon the only enemies named by the bishop who were already among the justices were Mark Slader and Robert Winter of Exeter. Slader is known only for the fact that he was one of the gentlemen who had been so ineffective in putting down the riot at Sampford Courtenay on Whit Monday, 1549. In fact, he does not appear to have been a justice at this time; and Robert Midwinter, if it was he, mayor in 1559-1560, was a man of Protestant inclinations but who had resisted Bishop Alley's attempts to be included within the city's magistracy! Not mentioned by the bishop were other leading Exeter citizens who, although not overtly antagonistic, still preferred the old faith; among these was John Wolcott, mayor in 1565-1566. Clearly, this was a list of victims rather personal to the bishop.

Alley also mentioned Christopher Coplestone, not as an enemy but as one not fit to be a magistrate "by the reason of divers disorders." The Coplestones were a very old landed gentry family that had been living somewhat in the shade for a couple of generations. Of the remainder of the magistrates, the bishop found many of them not as "earnest" as he would have liked but nevertheless needed on the bench for their learning, knowledge, and wisdom. Those he warned should not be made justices were John Arundell of Lanherne; Francis Tregian, John Tremayne, John Treguddick, John Hill, and William Cavell of Cornwall; and, for Devon, Richard Hert, the town clerk of Exeter, a Mr. Flear, and a Mr. Kirkham of Pinhoe near Exeter. Hert was possibly a personal antagonist, but the Kirkhams were later recusants. Most were, of course, the precursors of the later Catholic recusants, for Alley, like Bedford, if not exactly a Puritan, was what he would have called a "godly" man, perhaps even a supporter of a preaching ministry. All in all it would appear that in Alley's estimation the queen had few enemies, on account of their religion, in the South West.

And so it continued, so far as Catholics were concerned, throughout Elizabeth's reign. In 1569 James Courtenay, justice of the peace, of the branch of that family seated in Molland, refused to declare his assent to the Act of Uniformity but resolutely declared his loyalty to the queen. His fellow magistrates continually assured the Privy Council that the South West was in good order. Nearly a decade later, on November 30, 1577, at Launceston in Cornwall, Cuthbert Mayne became the first Roman Catholic priest to be executed; this points only to the recusancy of a few very isolated families, in this case the Arundells of Lanherne. The identification at about this time of a Tremayne, a Gilbert, a Bassett, a Wyatt, a Pollard, a Drewe, and even a Carew among young West Country men with Catholic tendencies at the London inns of court does not necessarily indicate widespread dissent within their families. Mayne had become a Catholic at Oxford, had followed Edmund Campion to Douai, and had only returned to England in 1576. The sheriff responsible for his arrest was Richard Grenville (he was knighted later that same year), and Mayne had no hope of escape. Mayne's execution was also the death knell for Cornish Catholicism. Two years later the Privy Council thanked the justices of Devon and Cornwall for their good work in containing potential "enemies." It seems very unlikely that the various schemes to send groups of Catholics to set up their own colonies in the New World would have received much support in the South West. To some extent this was attributable to Bishop John Woolton (1579-1594), who, although a man more likely to tolerate Puritan than Catholic nonconformity, did not believe in unnecessary harassment. In 1586, following the uncovering of the Babington Conspiracy, in which Ralegh played a not altogether honorable though perhaps profitable role, one of those arrested and later released was Sir William Kirkham. He was one of a handful of Devonians named in 1588, possibly by Ralegh, as potentially unreliable, but he lived until 1620, having by then inherited the estate of his elder brother at Blagdon near Paignton.

An inquiry carried out in 1592 found no new recusant names in Devon, but that same year the government got wind that the Spaniards were expecting support from Sir William Courtenay should they succeed in effecting a landing. Nevertheless, Courtenay was neither inhibited from taking the Devon musters that year nor from administering, with Sir Francis Drake, Sir John Gilbert, and the sheriff, Richard Champernowne, the Oath of Supremacy to the Devon justices. In 1596 Courtenay married Sir Francis Drake's widow, Elizabeth, and in 1601 he once again represented Devon in parliament. An Irishman, James Doudal, was executed in Exeter in 1598 for denying the queen's supremacy, but Courtenay continued to serve as a deputy lieutenant until 1614, although by then he was a notorious church papist, that is, one who no longer received Anglican holy communion. His third wife was a known Catholic recusant. Had there been a greater or growing number like them in Elizabethan Devon, more determined efforts presumably would have been made to inflict harsher penalties than fines and occasional temporary imprisonment. In 1603 a survey by Bishop Cotton listed only ninety-nine recusants in Devon and Cornwall, of whom fifty-five were women. Recusants constituted at this time a mere 5 percent of the total number of communicants, but their number, in a more tolerant climate, would soon increase.[30]

It must be remembered that by no means all committed Protestants had gone into exile during Mary Tudor's reign. While the young Thomas Bodley was taken by his father, an Exeter merchant, to Geneva, whence they returned in 1558 to settle in London, John Hooker, an Exeter man of radical religious views, thought public order more important even than religion and stayed behind to accept office as city chamberlain under a Catholic mayor.

Walter Ralegh senior, who had suffered for his Protestantism at the hands of the rebels in 1549, also found life in Devon more profitable than exile, but he took a risk in 1554 in arranging for Sir Peter Carew and others to escape by boat from Weymouth. He had been a Protestant pacesetter as early as 1546 when, so it is said, he broke up and kept a silver-gilt cross from East Budleigh church valued at £60. His wife Katherine also risked trouble in 1558 by visiting a convicted Protestant heretic, Agnes Prest, from the parish of Boyton near Launceston in Cornwall, as the woman lay in an Exeter prison, and comforting her, it was said, with the convictions "that God dwelleth not in temples made with hands" and that the situation that then existed would not last much longer. Katherine Ralegh clearly felt humbled by this poor illiterate countrywoman, and her four-year-old son Walter must have been aware both of his mother's courage and of her horrifying experience. But all that was very soon behind them, as Katherine had foretold. There is some rather slender evidence that Walter senior served as churchwarden of East Budleigh in 1561. Be that as it may, there was probably no widespread and headlong rush to remove what to him must have been very offensive images and other church furnishings.

In a diocese in which there were many parish priests still alive at Elizabeth's accession who had been admitted to their cures before the Henrician breach with Rome, the new settlement was just one more set of changes to which they and their flocks had to accommodate themselves. As before, they dragged their feet and avoided further expense as long as they dared. Even the returning Marian exiles failed, even if they all tried, to persuade many of the clergy either to preach or to forsake the traditional vestments, but in Bishops Alley, Bradbridge, and Woolton they found allies in promoting priests more to their liking when opportunities arose and no great enthusiasm for depriving priests with moderately Puritan inclinations.

Puritanism, at least in Devon, unlike Catholicism, appeared in certain quite discernible areas, especially in parishes whose patronage lay with Francis, earl of Bedford.[31] Perhaps the most important of the earl's promotions was that of John Travers, brother of Walter, the well-known Puritan leader, to Farringdon, north of East Budleigh, in about 1579. Early in Elizabeth's reign "godliness" was most pronounced in north Devon, in Barnstaple and the many parishes north and east of the town, including Sir John Chichester's parish of Shirwell. In fact the part played by gentlemen in that area is clearly demonstrated by the contents of a letter written, in Pauline fashion, in 1562 by a William Ramsay to his former parishioners at South Molton. Ramsay sent his greetings not only to Sir John Chichester but also to Richard Fortescue of Filleigh (then sheriff of Devon), Lewis

Pollard of King's Nympton, John Parker of North Molton, and other gentlemen in this area.

More than twenty years later, people from Barnstaple made new-style pilgrimages to Pilton, another Chichester parish, to hear, as the town clerk mockingly reported, "a trental of sermons." "They called [it] an exercise or holy fast," he added, "and there some offered as they did when they went on a pilgrimage," this being a relief, no doubt, to the churchwardens, for Pilton church had suffered a considerable financial loss when its shrine had been dismantled in Henry VIII's reign. Shirwell too was a popular godly venue, and it was later complained of Richard Burton, who was presented to the church there by Sir John Chichester in 1580, that, among other things, he refused to wear a surplice, which he called "a popish rag"; omitted the ring in the marriage ceremony; allowed people to stand to receive the sacrament; and neglected to read the Epistle, Gospels, Litany, *Benedictus, Te Deum,* and the psalms. Ironically, the Catholic martyr Cuthbert Mayne had been born in this same north Devon parish back in 1544. Even Sir John's death in 1586 did not alter things, for under his son's patronage Pilton also acquired a Puritan "lecturer." It is no wonder the more conformist earl of Bath strove to hold his own in Barnstaple, but even he could not prevent the town from appointing its own brand of preachers.

Another Puritan area lay in the harsh country in northwest Devon centered on Holsworthy and stretching over into the Grenville parish of Kilkhampton in Cornwall. Humphrey Speccot, esquire, presented Puritan clergy to Thornbury, Milton Damerell, Tetcott, and possibly to Hollacombe between 1573 and 1591. To Thornbury in 1573 came the man who was to emerge later as the leader of the Puritan clergy in Devon—Melanchthon Jewell. These parishes are known about only because their Puritan incumbents were deprived in the great purge of 1603. Until then there was little local clerical leadership or organization, nor indeed systematic repression.

But trouble did occur much earlier in at least one rather unlooked-for quarter. In 1580 Sir Richard Grenville, not otherwise known as a particularly zealous Protestant but apparently in the full knowledge of what he was doing, presented to Kilkhampton one Eusebius Paget, an undoubtedly "godly" but also very troublesome clergyman who had already been deprived by the bishop of Peterborough for preaching against the use of the Book of Common Prayer. Bishop Woolton knew of his history and, according to Paget, promised to be tolerant. By 1583, if not before, Grenville bitterly regretted the appointment, especially when in that year he was himself upbraided by Lord Hastings, a radical Puritan who had known Paget in Leicestershire, for not appreciating the parson's plain speaking. "The man whom the Lord hath thoroughly seasoned with humility he falleth flat before the sceptre of the word and yieldeth to be censured by it, as a mean to reform him," Hastings wrote. If this was how Paget addressed Grenville, it was no wonder he was thrown out, for humility was hardly his patron's forte.

Paget went off to Barnstaple, where he caused more trouble, among other things discouraging the singing of hymns and the playing of the organ. He also preached from half past ten until one o'clock. He had his following in Barnstaple but also his enemies, for, according to a complaint by the curate there against this man, who after all was not the incumbent, "People when they are married, woman great with child, Her Majesty's subjects lying at the point of death, mariners and travellers going to sea, have all been denied and put back from receiving the Communion, to the great distress of her poor subjects' consciences." Meanwhile, not only was Grenville also called to account by no less a person than Sir Francis Walsingham for evicting Paget, but he could not get rid of Mrs. Paget, her family, and her friends—two of them a Scot and his wife—from the parsonage. One of the more interesting details of the business is that Grenville began an action for trespass against Mrs. Paget in the stannary court, only to be frustrated by a Bodmin lawyer and justice, John Kempthorne, acting for the lady. The whole business must have been very exasperating indeed for the great explorer, with so many other uses for his time and patience.

By then, that is, the mid-1580s, there were about 100 "preaching" clergy in the 600 parishes of the diocese, but the Puritans themselves recognized only about one tenth of them as really "godly" preachers. By 1603 there were more than 200 judged by the less rigorous criteria. Bishop John Woolton's biggest problem was the reappearance of the fringe sect known as the Family of Love. In 1582 the bishop wrote to Cecil: "I find your opinion by experience true that lenity will nothing prevail with these contentious persons. Therefore according to your lordship's counsel and in hope of your assistance, since the lamb's skin will do no good I will make trial how the lion's will prevail."

On the whole Woolton could count on the majority of the justices and other gentlemen to support him in curbing the excesses of Puritan fervor, but what mattered to them above all was public order. In 1595, under the chairmanship of Woolton's successor, Gervase Babington (1594-1597), the Devon magistrates declared their opposition to "church and parish ales, revels, May-games, plays," etc., and although they described these as a "great profanation of the Lord's Sabbath," they were not being especially Puritanical but meant what they said, namely that these were "a special cause that many disorders, contempts of law and other enormities are then perpetrated and committed . . . to the great hurt of the commonwealth." When they proceeded to forbid any drinking at any time on the Sabbath, during church services on any festival, or during the "night season," one wonders indeed whether such bylaws applied to all classes.

What emerges is a picture of a society tolerant of a good deal of nonconformity, short of any threat, real or potential, to the queen's peace. It was not so much religious fanaticism as abhorrence of the abuse of power that led Sir Arthur Champernowne, following the St. Bartholomew's Day Massacre in France in 1572, to write to the queen offering to find sixty "younger brothers to gentlemen, mean gentlemen being heirs, franklins [freeholders] and other lusty young fellows, all unmarried, the worst of them having in annuities and other yearly profits £20," as well as 500 foot soldiers at 8d the day, to go to the relief of Rochelle. On the whole, he and his fellow West Country gentlemen were, like the queen, reluctant to penalize men for their private religious beliefs, a feeling quite clearly shared by Sir Walter Ralegh when he spoke out, in the parliament of 1593, against what he regarded as draconian measures to rid the realm of Catholics and Puritans: "What danger may grow to ourselves if this law pass it were fit to be considered."

One does, however, detect, here and there among the southwestern gentry, a certain intellectual curiosity about religion. Was it not perhaps this that had moved Sir Richard Grenville in the early 1580s to invite Paget and his friends to lecture in his house to a group that we are told included his fellow member of parliament and deputy lieutenant, Sir William Mohun? Indeed, for a short while Paget ran a school for gentlemen's sons in Kilkhampton, until Grenville thought better of it. Sir Walter Ralegh, no doubt, would have enjoyed the domestic gatherings and possibly shocked those present, as he and his brother Carew are supposed to have shocked some of his Dorset acquaintances with their daring skepticism. In fact, of course, Ralegh, like most Elizabethans, was a thoroughly orthodox "Anglican" at heart, but he and Grenville and all other Englishmen interested in exploring the terrestrial globe were of necessity keen to learn from the new race of astrologers and mathematicians who explored the heavens, about which Christianity could tell them little. There were still many in high places who regarded forecasting the weather as sorcery. Ralegh's West Country cousins did not lack imagination, but unlike him they wrote little poetry. The more intellectual among them were given rather to the study of the law than to philosophy. Even Ralegh, who in tranquillity could write courtly prose, could write business letters as clumsy as those of any country knight. Although neither of them lived to read his *Historie of the World,* the two West Country men with whom Ralegh would probably have had most common ground toward the end of his life were Richard Carew and John Hooker. Both looked upon him as their patron, and it was Hooker's misfortune that the manuscript of his "Synopsis Chorographical" of the county of Devon came into Ralegh's hands at a time when his commendation would have carried little weight. Perhaps its publication is one of Ralegh's unfinished West Country tasks, which his fellow countrymen of the second Elizabethan age should take in hand.

Notes

[1]P. L. Hull (ed.), "Richard Carew's Discourse about the Duchy Suit, 1594," *Journal of the Royal Institution of Cornwall*, 1962, especially pp. 217-218.

[2]R. Carew, *Survey of Cornwall*, first edition, 1602. All quotations here follow the modernized text in F. E. Halliday (ed.), *Richard Carew of Anthony*, 1953.

[3]Devon Record Office, Exeter, Rolle Mss, 96/M/32.

[4]A. J. Howard and T. L. Stoate (eds.), *The Devon Muster Roll for 1569*, 1977, and M. M. Rowe and A. M. Jackson, (eds.), *Exeter Freemen 1266-1967*, D[evon and] C[ornwall] R[ecord] S[ociety], 1973.

[5]From a printed license by Ralegh to Philip Haywood of Lyme Regis, Dorset, vintner, and his daughter Joan, wife of George Sommer, in the Raleigh Collection in the Library of the University of North Carolina at Chapel Hill.

[6]This letter is now in the Devon Record Office.

[7]These family details have been compiled, except where otherwise stated, from the following: T. N. Brushfield, a series of articles in the *T[ransactions of the] D[evonshire] A[ssociation]*, 1889-1896; J. L. Vivian, *The Visitations of the County of Devon*, 1895; M. J. G. Stanford, "A History of the Ralegh Family of Fardel and Budleigh in the early Tudor period," unpublished M.A. thesis, University of London, 1955.

[8]J. Sheail, "The Distribution of Taxable Population and Wealth in England during the early sixteenth century," *Transactions of the Institute of British Geographers*, 1972.

[9]P. Slack, "Some Aspects of Epidemics in England," University of Oxford, D. Phil. thesis, 1972, and the same author's *The Impact of Plague in Tudor and Stuart England*, 1985.

[10]M. Cash (ed.), *Devon Inventories of the Sixteenth and Seventeenth Centuries*, D.C.R.S. 1966, pp. 10-11.

[11]There are several manuscript versions of Hooker's text, a small portion of the one in the British Library (Harl. Manuscripts 5827) having been printed in W. J. Blake, "Hooker's Synopsis Chorographical of Devonshire," *T.D.A.*, 1915. All quotations here have been modernized.

[12]From Sir Simon D'Ewes's *Journal* (1682), quoted in P. W. Hasler, *The House of Commons, 1558-1603*, 1981, II, p. 275, hereinafter cited as Hasler, *The House of Commons*.

[13]Hasler, *The House of Commons*, pp. 275-276.

[14]E. Edwards, *Life of Sir Walter Raleigh*, 1868, II, pp. 211-212, hereinafter cited as Edwards, *Life of Raleigh*, and T. A. P. Greeves, "The Devon Tin Industry," unpublished Ph.D. thesis, University of Exeter, 1981, pp. 45, 119.

[15]M. J. G. Stanford, "The Raleghs take to the Sea," *Mariner's Mirror*, 1962, passim.

[16]M. Oppenheim, *The Maritime History of Devon*, 1968, pp. 38-40, and A. L. Rowse, *Tudor Cornwall*, 1941, pp. 69-70, hereinafter cited as *Tudor Cornwall*.

[17]P. Russell, *Dartmouth*, 1950, especially pp. 63-71.

[18]T. S. Willan, *Studies in Elizabethan Trade*, 1959, pp. 79-82.

[19]J. R. Chanter, *Sketches of the History of Barnstaple,* 1865, pp. 96-98, and K. R. Andrews, *Elizabethan Privateering,* 1964, p. 103.

[20]N. J. G. Pounds (ed.), *The Parliamentary Survey of the Duchy of Cornwall,* D.C.R.S., 1982, pp. xix-xx.

[21]J. A. Youings (ed.), *Devon Monastic Lands,* D.C.R.S., 1955, pp. 19-20, 45-47, and J. E. Kew, "The Land Market in Devon 1536-58," unpublished Ph.D. thesis, University of Exeter, 1967, pp. 285-298, hereinafter cited as Kew, "The Land Market in Devon."

[22]J. Barber, "Sir Francis Drake's Investments in Plymouth property," *T.D.A.,* 1981.

[23]Kew, "The Land Market in Devon," pp. 266-281.

[24]D. B. Quinn, *The Elizabethans and the Irish,* 1966, p. 115.

[25]J. Roberts, "The Armada Lord Lieutenant," *T.D.A.,* 1970 and 1971.

[26]A. L. Rowse, *Sir Richard Grenville,* 1937, and *Tudor Cornwall;* J. A. Youings, *Early Tudor Exeter,* 1974, and Edwards, *Life of Raleigh,* II, 36-38.

[27]Edwards, *Life of Raleigh,* II, p. 39, and Rowse, *Tudor Cornwall,* p. 396.

[28]Edwards, *Life of Raleigh,* II, pp. 112-117.

[29]The material used for this section is very largely from Hasler, *The House of Commons.*

[30]For the Catholics of Cornwall, see Rowse, *Tudor Cornwall,* Chapter XIV. The Devon Catholics still await their historian, but see J. Roberts, "A notable Devon knight: Sir William Courtenay, 1553-1630," *T.D.A.,* 1956.

[31]I. Gowers, "Puritanism in Devon," unpublished M.A. thesis, University of Exeter, 1970. For the response of the parishes of Devon and Cornwall to the religious changes up to 1570, see R. Whiting, "The Reformation in the South West of England," unpublished Ph.D. thesis, University of Exeter, 1977.